BROKEN
——— BEYOND ———
RECOGNITION
Prayer Journal

Beauty from Ashes

Katherine Elam Simpson

Largo, MD

This Journal Belongs to

_____

Copyright © 2020 Katherine Elam Simpson

All rights reserved under the international copyright law. No part of this book may be reproduced or transmitted in any form or by any means, electronic or mechanical, including photocopying, recording, or by any information storage and retrieval system, without the express, written permission of the publisher or the author. The exception is reviewers, who may quote brief passages in a review.

ISBN 9781562293932

Christian Living Books, Inc.
P. O. Box 7584
Largo, MD 20792
christianlivingbooks.com
We bring your dreams to fruition.

Unless otherwise noted, Scripture quotations are taken from the King James Version of the Bible. Scripture quotations marked NIV are taken from the Holy Bible, New International Version®, NIV®. Copyright © 1973, 1978, 1984, 2011 by Biblica, Inc.® Used by permission of Zondervan. All rights reserved worldwide. Scripture quotations marked NKJV are taken from the New King James Version®. Copyright © 1982 by Thomas Nelson. Used by permission. All rights reserved. Scripture quotations marked NLT are taken from the Holy Bible, New Living Translation, Copyright © 1996, 2004, 2007 by Tyndale House Foundation. Used by permission of Tyndale House Publishers, Inc. All rights reserved.

Introduction

This prayer journal is dedicated to those seeking a closer walk with Jesus Christ. As I said in my book, *Broken Beyond Recognition*, I wasn't supposed to be an author. But to God be the glory. I have defeated the odds of illiteracy, alcoholism, prostitution, drug abuse, physical abuse, mental abuse, and childhood trauma. How? Primarily by praying.

> *Don't worry about anything; instead, pray about everything. Tell God what you need, and thank him for all he has done.*
> (Philippians 4:6 NKJV)

> *Then you will call on me and come and pray to me, and I will listen to you.*
> (Jeremiah 29:12 NLT)

God is constantly working to bring us all to the place of brokenness. It is not to hurt us but to help us! Sometimes there is a sudden breaking. Other times it can be daily trials, hard circumstances, physical problems, and all sorts of things to bring us to a place of brokenness. But be sure, He's not only in the business of lovingly breaking us but also sweeping up all the broken pieces and molding them back together for His greater purpose.

The Lord is close to the brokenhearted and saves those who are crushed in spirit.
(Psalm 34:18 NIV)

My sacrifice, O God, is a broken spirit; a broken and contrite heart, you God will not despise. (Psalm 51:17)

I will never forget the day the Lord gave me surgical instructions on how to become free. He instructed me to do four things: pray, repent, forgive and release the past. I encourage you to follow that formula each and every day. Do the work to effect the change you seek. Be intentional. Be consistent.

This is a resource to help you realize the greatness God has placed in all of us. I want to let you know that nothing can stop it! Every time you are attacked, hit hard, and hurt, run to God in prayer. Allow Him to heal and restore you. If you read my book, I hope my journey inspired you to see that if God transformed my life, He can do it for you as well.

But He heals the brokenhearted and binds their wounds. (Psalms 147:3 NKJV)

Spiritual Goal

Brokenness tames our spirit to trust God.

Start Date: Achieve by:

Describe Your Spiritual Goal   **Progress Check**

Actionable Steps   **Reason for This Goal**

- ○
- ○
- ○
- ○
- ○
- ○

Challenges   Notes:

Brokenness Brings Hope

Date: _____

Bible Study, Meditation & Memory Verses

Gratitude & Praise to God: _____
_____
_____
_____
_____
_____
_____
_____
_____

Brokenness Reflections

Big Goals and Dreams

Repentance and Forgiveness

Prayer Requests: _____
_____
_____
_____
_____
_____
_____
_____
_____
_____

Answered Prayers: _____
_____
_____
_____
_____
_____

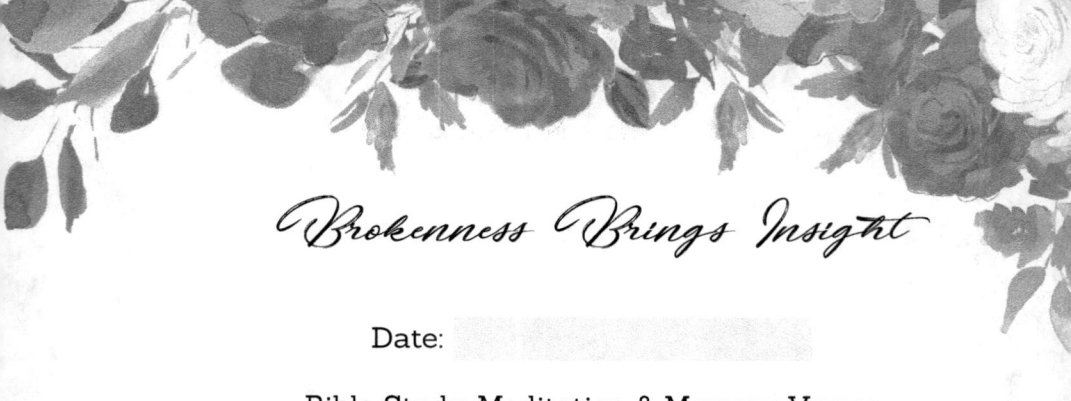

Brokenness Brings Insight

Date: _____

Bible Study, Meditation & Memory Verses

Gratitude & Praise to God: _____
_____
_____
_____
_____
_____
_____
_____

Brokenness Reflections

Big Goals and Dreams

Repentance and Forgiveness

Prayer Requests: _____
_____
_____
_____
_____
_____
_____
_____
_____
_____

Answered Prayers: _____
_____
_____
_____
_____
_____
_____

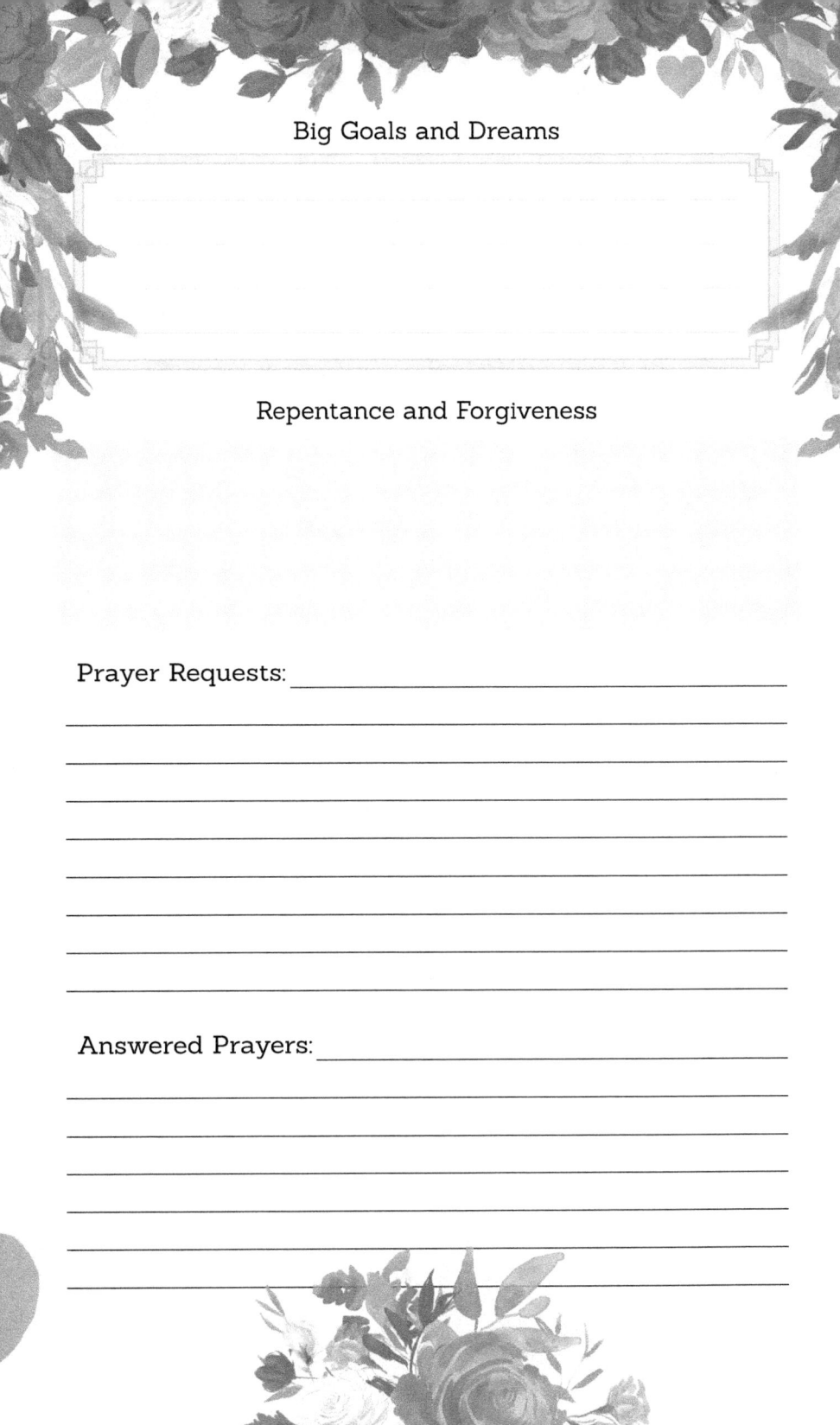

Brokenness Brings Serenity

Date: _____

Bible Study, Meditation & Memory Verses

Gratitude & Praise to God: _____
_____
_____
_____
_____
_____
_____
_____

Brokenness Reflections

Big Goals and Dreams

Repentance and Forgiveness

Prayer Requests: _____
_____
_____
_____
_____
_____
_____
_____
_____

Answered Prayers: _____
_____
_____
_____
_____
_____
_____

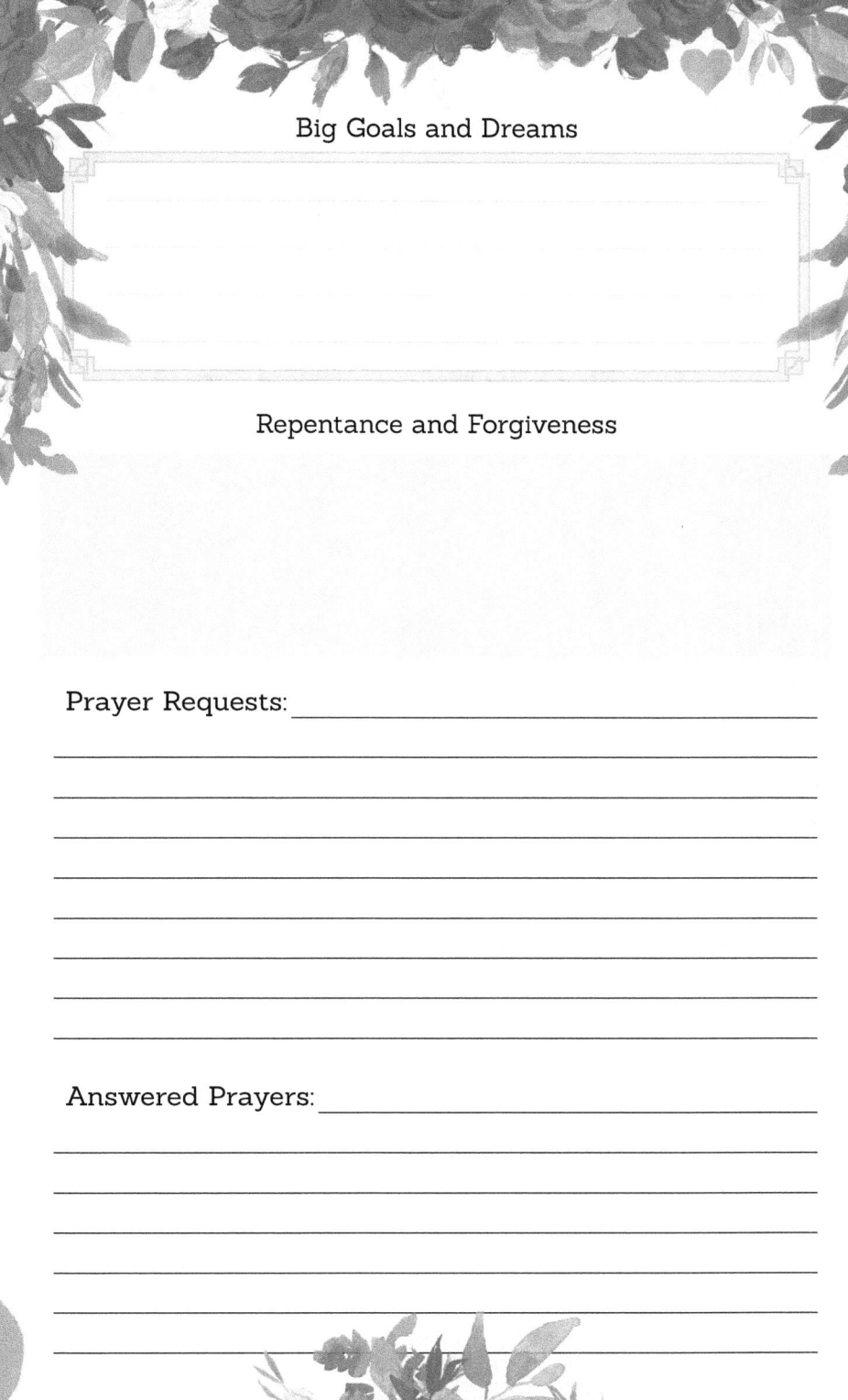

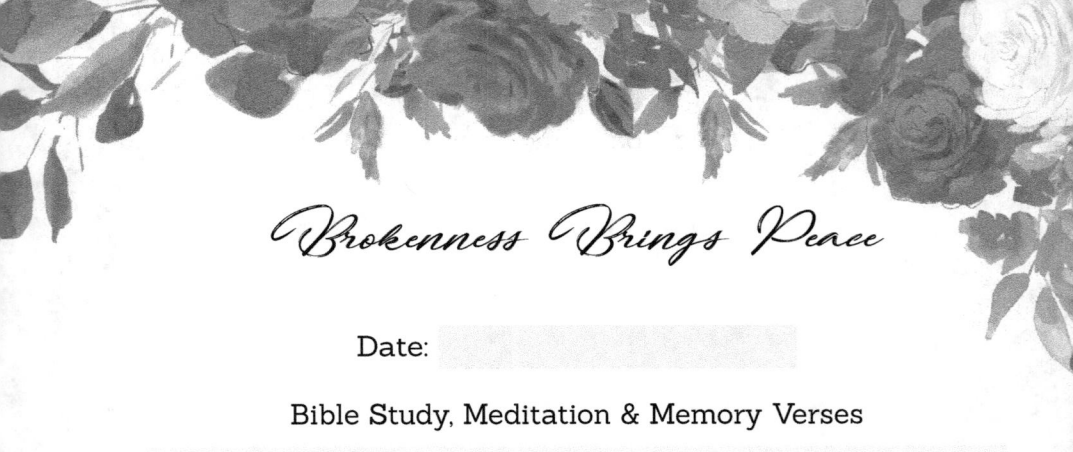

Brokenness Brings Peace

Date: _____

Bible Study, Meditation & Memory Verses

Gratitude & Praise to God: _____
_____
_____
_____
_____
_____
_____
_____

Brokenness Reflections

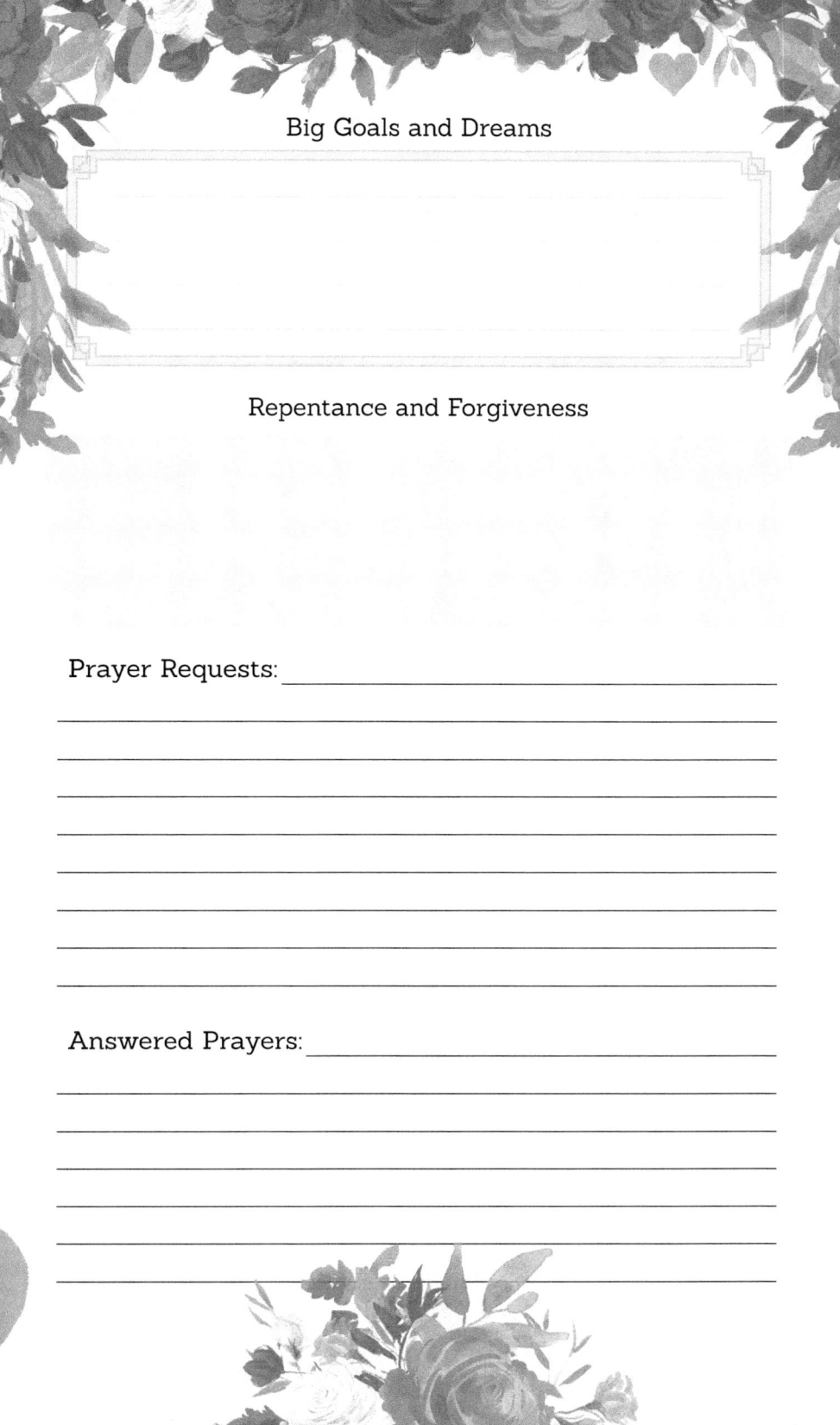

Big Goals and Dreams

Repentance and Forgiveness

Prayer Requests: _____
_____
_____
_____
_____
_____
_____
_____
_____
_____

Answered Prayers: _____
_____
_____
_____
_____
_____
_____

Brokenness Brings Agape Love

Date: _____

Bible Study, Meditation & Memory Verses

Gratitude & Praise to God: _____
_____
_____
_____
_____
_____
_____
_____
_____

Brokenness Reflections

Big Goals and Dreams

Repentance and Forgiveness

Prayer Requests: _____
_____
_____
_____
_____
_____
_____
_____
_____
_____

Answered Prayers: _____
_____
_____
_____
_____
_____

Brokenness Brings Compassion

Date: _____

Bible Study, Meditation & Memory Verses

Gratitude & Praise to God: _____
_____
_____
_____
_____
_____
_____
_____

Brokenness Reflections

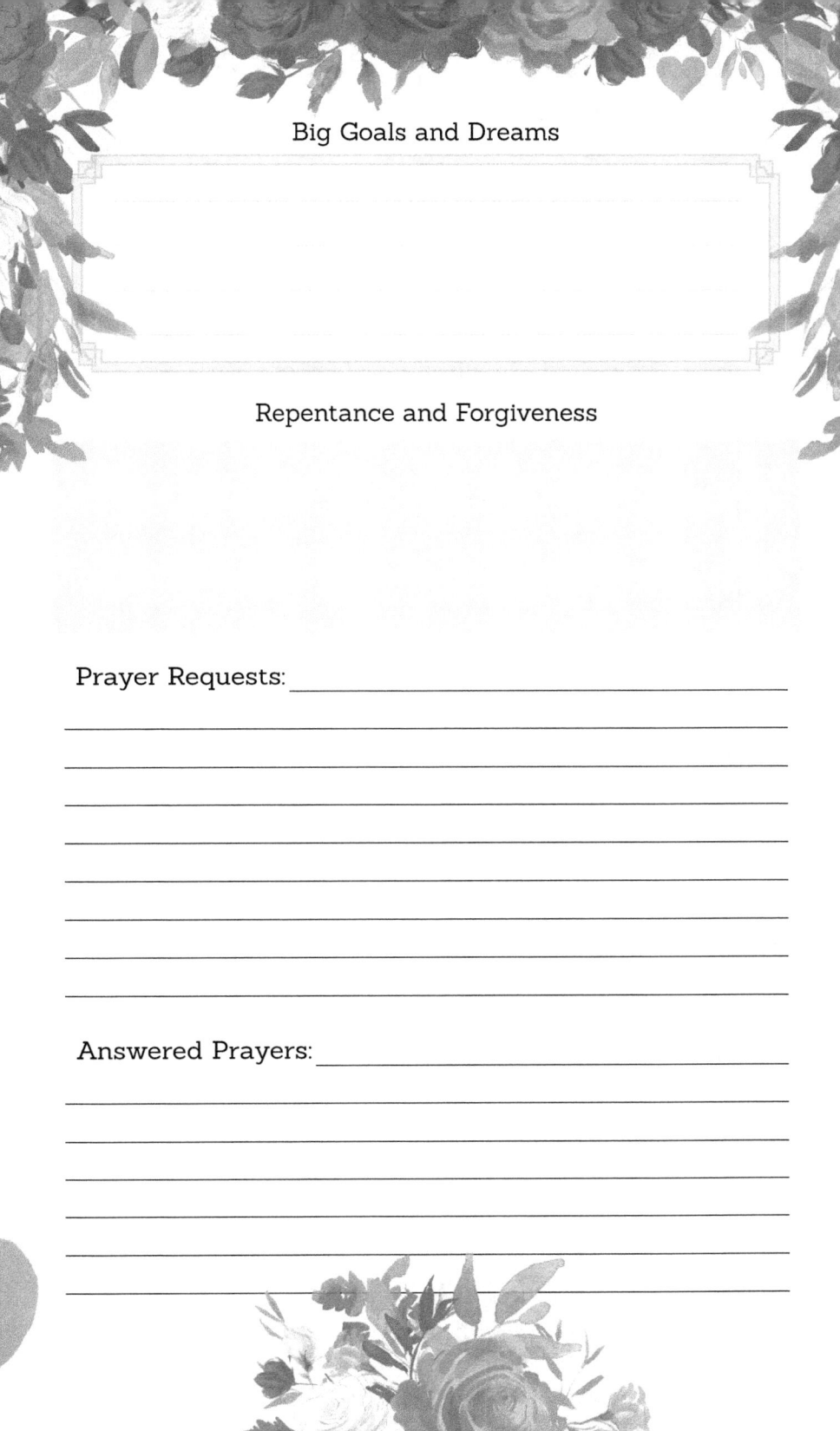

Big Goals and Dreams

Repentance and Forgiveness

Prayer Requests: _____
_____
_____
_____
_____
_____
_____
_____
_____
_____

Answered Prayers: _____
_____
_____
_____
_____
_____
_____
_____

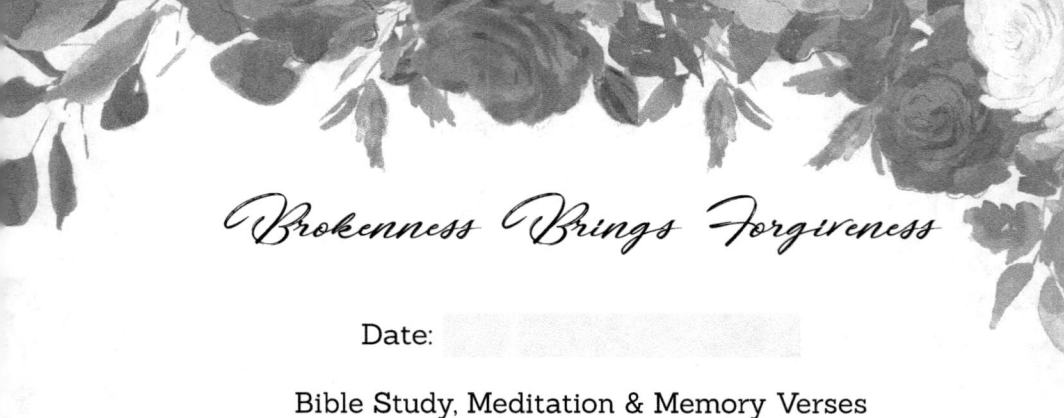

Brokenness Brings Forgiveness

Date: _____

Bible Study, Meditation & Memory Verses

Gratitude & Praise to God: _____
_____
_____
_____
_____
_____
_____
_____
_____

Brokenness Reflections

Big Goals and Dreams

Repentance and Forgiveness

Prayer Requests: _____
_____
_____
_____
_____
_____
_____
_____
_____
_____

Answered Prayers: _____
_____
_____
_____
_____
_____
_____

Brokenness Brings Unselfishness

Date: _____

Bible Study, Meditation & Memory Verses

Gratitude & Praise to God: _____
_____
_____
_____
_____
_____
_____
_____
_____

Brokenness Reflections

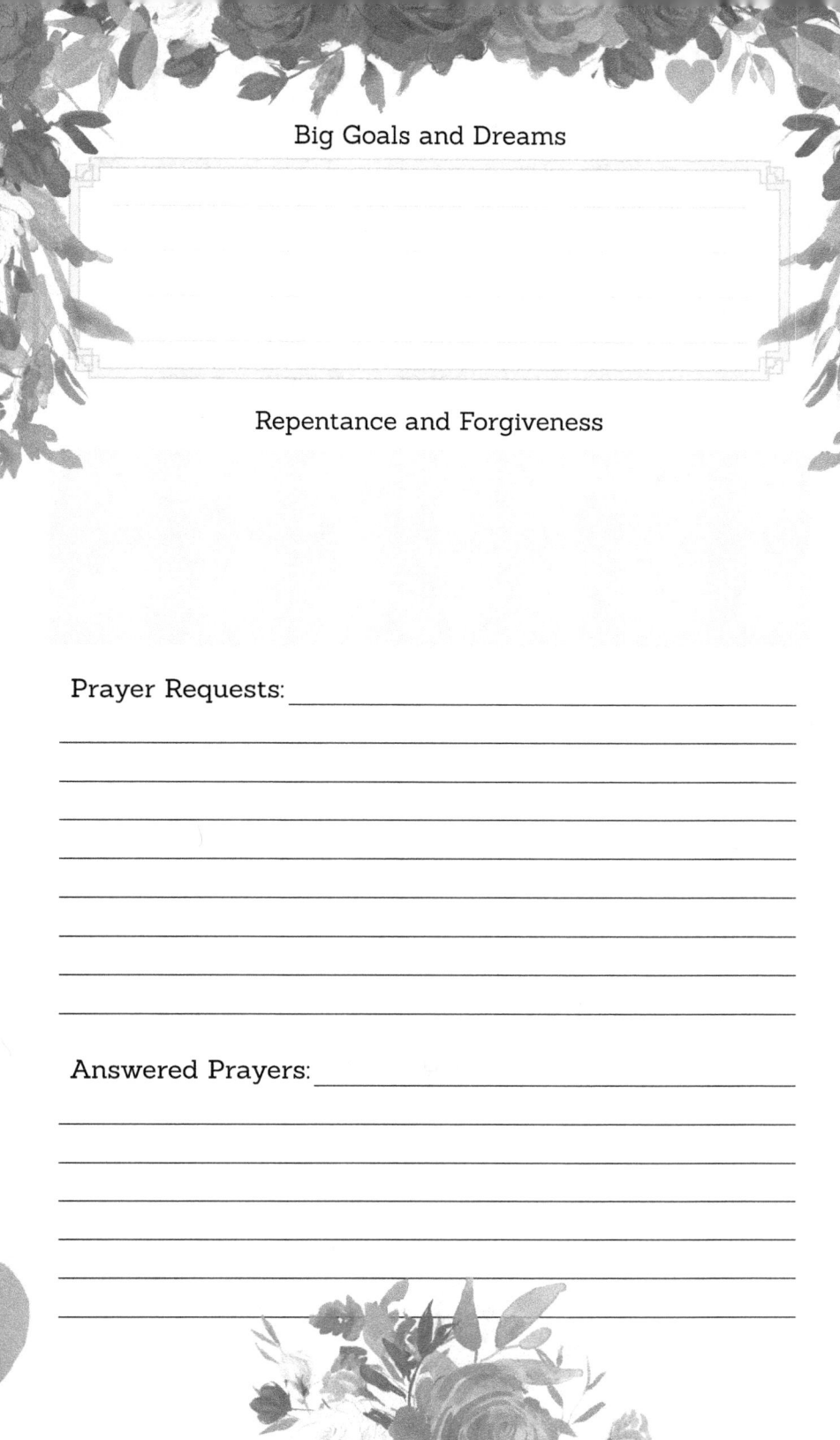

Big Goals and Dreams

Repentance and Forgiveness

Prayer Requests: _____
_____
_____
_____
_____
_____
_____
_____
_____
_____

Answered Prayers: _____
_____
_____
_____
_____
_____

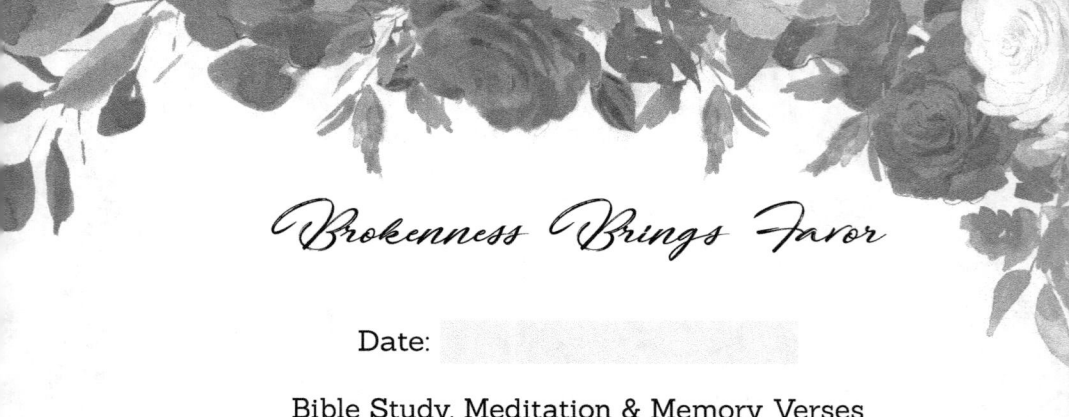

Brokenness Brings Favor

Date: _____

Bible Study, Meditation & Memory Verses

Gratitude & Praise to God: _____
_____
_____
_____
_____
_____
_____
_____

Brokenness Reflections

Big Goals and Dreams

Repentance and Forgiveness

Prayer Requests: _____
_____
_____
_____
_____
_____
_____
_____
_____
_____
_____

Answered Prayers: _____
_____
_____
_____
_____
_____
_____

Personal Goal

Brokenness gives us a bridge to cross over into God's love.

Start Date: _____ Achieve by: _____

Describe Your Personal Goal

Progress Check

Actionable Steps

- ☐
- ☐
- ☐
- ☐
- ☐
- ☐

Reason for This Goal

Challenges

Notes: _____

Brokenness Brings Patience

Date: _____

Bible Study, Meditation & Memory Verses

Gratitude & Praise to God: _____
_____
_____
_____
_____
_____
_____
_____
_____

Brokenness Reflections

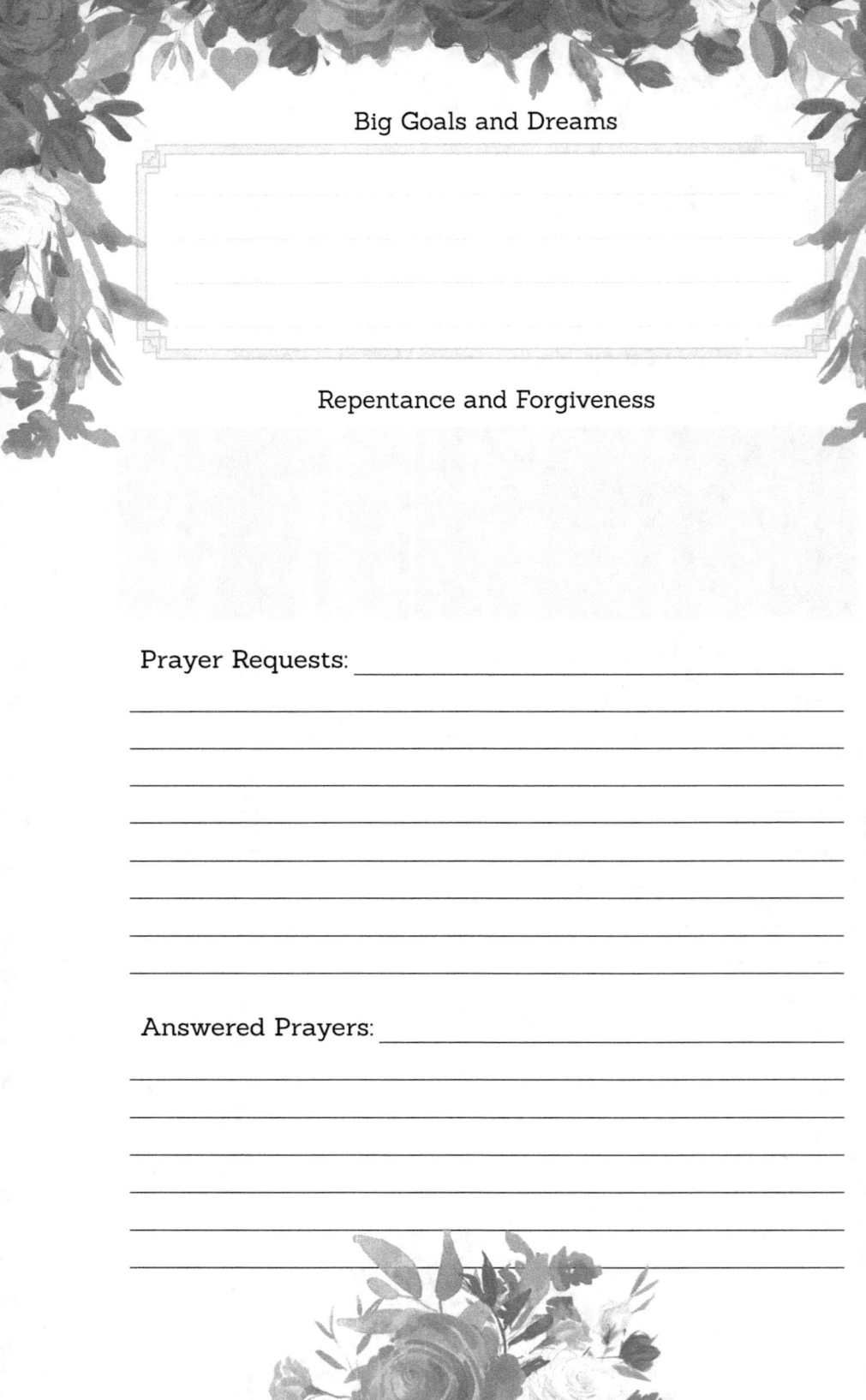

Big Goals and Dreams

Repentance and Forgiveness

Prayer Requests: _____

Answered Prayers: _____

Brokenness Brings Kindness

Date: _____

Bible Study, Meditation & Memory Verses

Gratitude & Praise to God: _____
_____
_____
_____
_____
_____
_____
_____

Brokenness Reflections

Big Goals and Dreams

Repentance and Forgiveness

Prayer Requests: _____
_____
_____
_____
_____
_____
_____
_____
_____

Answered Prayers: _____
_____
_____
_____
_____
_____
_____

Brokenness Brings Perseverance

Date: _____

Bible Study, Meditation & Memory Verses

Gratitude & Praise to God: _____
_____
_____
_____
_____
_____
_____
_____
_____

Brokenness Reflections

Big Goals and Dreams

Repentance and Forgiveness

Prayer Requests: _____
_____
_____
_____
_____
_____
_____
_____
_____
_____

Answered Prayers: _____
_____
_____
_____
_____
_____
_____

Brokenness Brings Truth

Date: _____

Bible Study, Meditation & Memory Verses

Gratitude & Praise to God: _____
_____
_____
_____
_____
_____
_____
_____

Brokenness Reflections

Big Goals and Dreams

Repentance and Forgiveness

Prayer Requests: _____

_____
_____
_____
_____
_____
_____
_____
_____
_____

Answered Prayers: _____

_____
_____
_____
_____
_____
_____

Brokenness Brings Renewal

Date: _____

Bible Study, Meditation & Memory Verses

Gratitude & Praise to God: _____
_____
_____
_____
_____
_____
_____
_____
_____

Brokenness Reflections

Big Goals and Dreams

Repentance and Forgiveness

Prayer Requests: _____
_____
_____
_____
_____
_____
_____
_____
_____
_____

Answered Prayers: _____
_____
_____
_____
_____
_____
_____

Brokenness Brings Cleansing

Date: _____

Bible Study, Meditation & Memory Verses

Gratitude & Praise to God: _____
_____
_____
_____
_____
_____
_____
_____

Brokenness Reflections

Big Goals and Dreams

Repentance and Forgiveness

Prayer Requests: _____
_____
_____
_____
_____
_____
_____
_____
_____
_____

Answered Prayers: _____
_____
_____
_____
_____
_____
_____

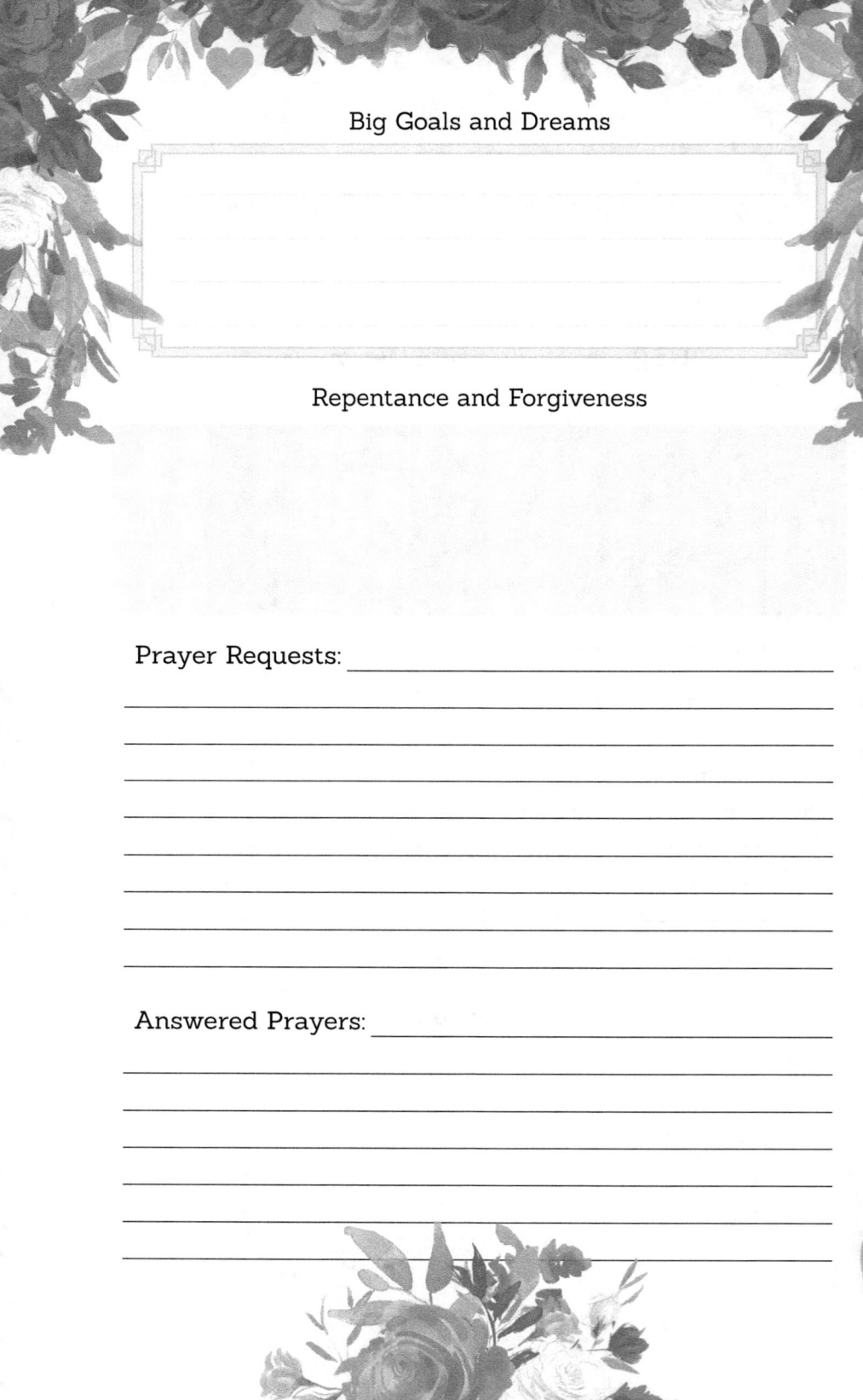

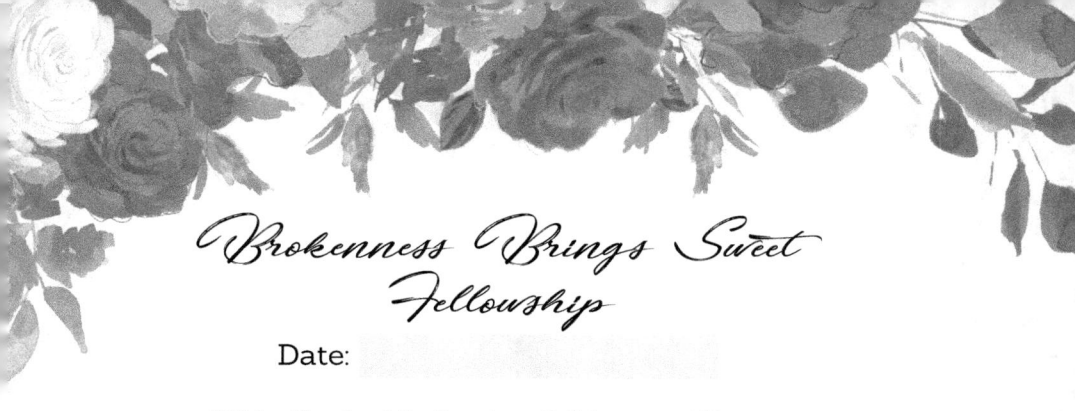

Brokenness Brings Sweet Fellowship

Date: _____

Bible Study, Meditation & Memory Verses

Gratitude & Praise to God: _____
_____
_____
_____
_____
_____
_____
_____

Brokenness Reflections

Big Goals and Dreams

Repentance and Forgiveness

Prayer Requests: _____
_____
_____
_____
_____
_____
_____
_____
_____
_____

Answered Prayers: _____
_____
_____
_____
_____
_____
_____
_____

Brokenness Brings Refreshing

Date:

Bible Study, Meditation & Memory Verses

Gratitude & Praise to God: _____
_____
_____
_____
_____
_____
_____
_____
_____

Brokenness Reflections

Big Goals and Dreams

Repentance and Forgiveness

Prayer Requests: _____
_____
_____
_____
_____
_____
_____
_____
_____
_____

Answered Prayers: _____
_____
_____
_____
_____
_____
_____

Brokenness Brings Meekness

Date:

Bible Study, Meditation & Memory Verses

Gratitude & Praise to God: _____
_____
_____
_____
_____
_____
_____
_____
_____

Brokenness Reflections

Big Goals and Dreams

Repentance and Forgiveness

Prayer Requests: _____
_____
_____
_____
_____
_____
_____
_____
_____
_____

Answered Prayers: _____
_____
_____
_____
_____
_____
_____

Brokenness Brings Praise

Date: _____

Bible Study, Meditation & Memory Verses

Gratitude & Praise to God: _____
_____
_____
_____
_____
_____
_____
_____
_____

Brokenness Reflections

Big Goals and Dreams

Repentance and Forgiveness

Prayer Requests: _____
_____
_____
_____
_____
_____
_____
_____
_____
_____

Answered Prayers: _____
_____
_____
_____
_____
_____
_____
_____

Relationship Goal

Brokenness causes a crushing that results in humility.

Start Date: _____   Achieve by: _____

Describe Your Relationship Goal
_____
_____
_____
_____

Progress Check

Actionable Steps
- ○
- ○
- ○
- ○
- ○
- ○

Reason for This Goal
_____
_____
_____
_____
_____

Challenges

Notes: _____
_____
_____
_____
_____
_____
_____

Brokenness Brings Worship

Date: _____

Bible Study, Meditation & Memory Verses

Gratitude & Praise to God: _____
_____
_____
_____
_____
_____
_____
_____
_____

Brokenness Reflections

Big Goals and Dreams

Repentance and Forgiveness

Prayer Requests: _____
_____
_____
_____
_____
_____
_____
_____
_____
_____
_____

Answered Prayers: _____
_____
_____
_____
_____
_____
_____

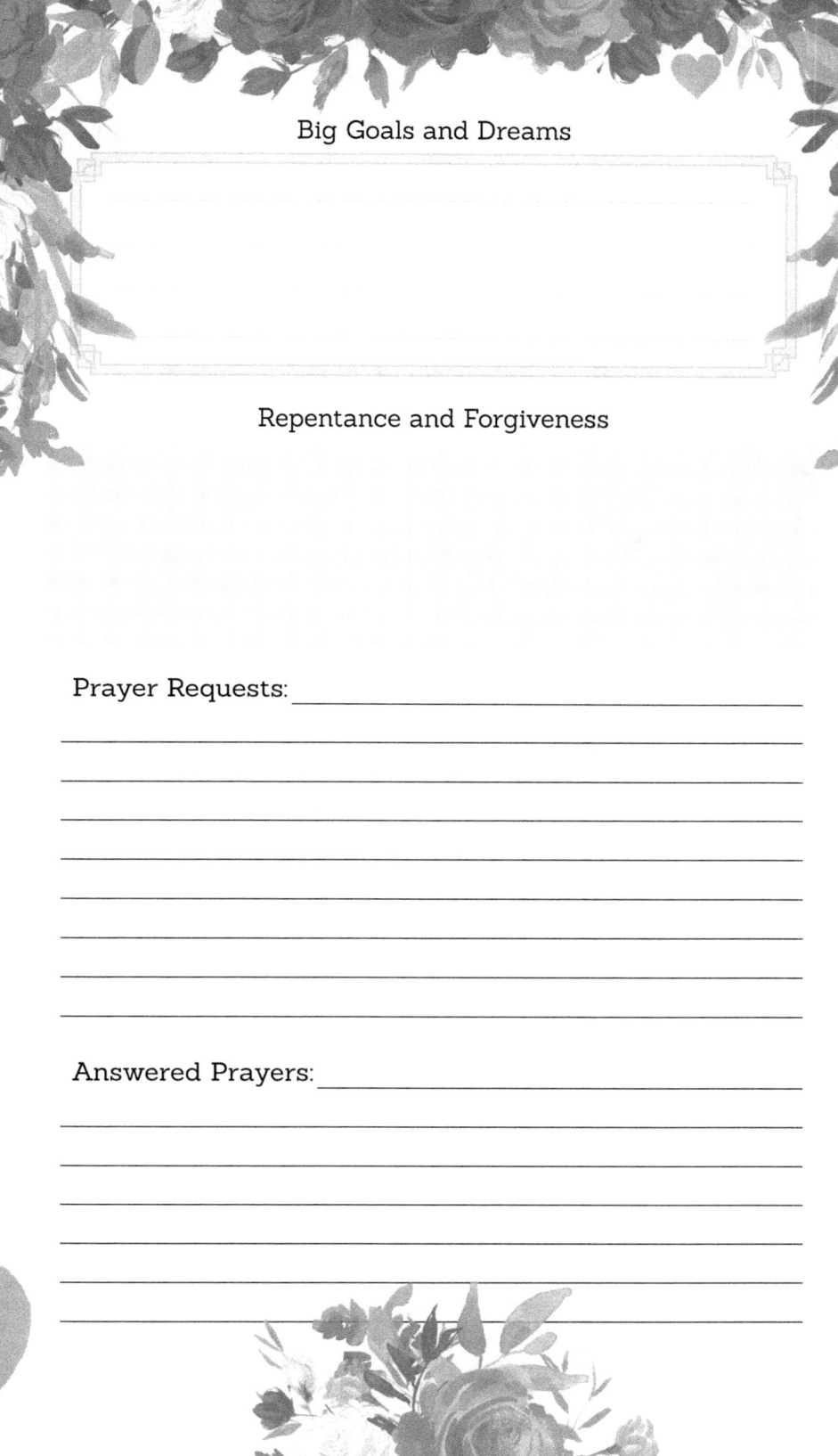

Brokenness Brings Longsuffering

Date: _____

Bible Study, Meditation & Memory Verses

Gratitude & Praise to God: _____
_____
_____
_____
_____
_____
_____
_____
_____

Brokenness Reflections

Big Goals and Dreams

Repentance and Forgiveness

Prayer Requests: _____

_____
_____
_____
_____
_____
_____
_____
_____
_____

Answered Prayers: _____

_____
_____
_____
_____
_____
_____

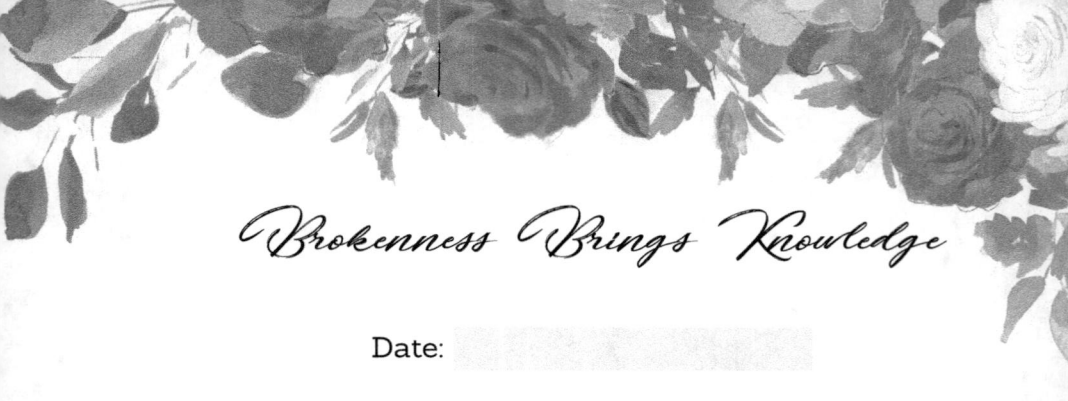

Brokenness Brings Knowledge

Date: _____

Bible Study, Meditation & Memory Verses

Gratitude & Praise to God: _____
_____
_____
_____
_____
_____
_____
_____
_____

Brokenness Reflections

Big Goals and Dreams

Repentance and Forgiveness

Prayer Requests: _____
_____
_____
_____
_____
_____
_____
_____
_____
_____

Answered Prayers: _____
_____
_____
_____
_____
_____
_____

Brokenness Brings Joy

Date: _____

Bible Study, Meditation & Memory Verses

Gratitude & Praise to God: _____
_____
_____
_____
_____
_____
_____
_____

Brokenness Reflections

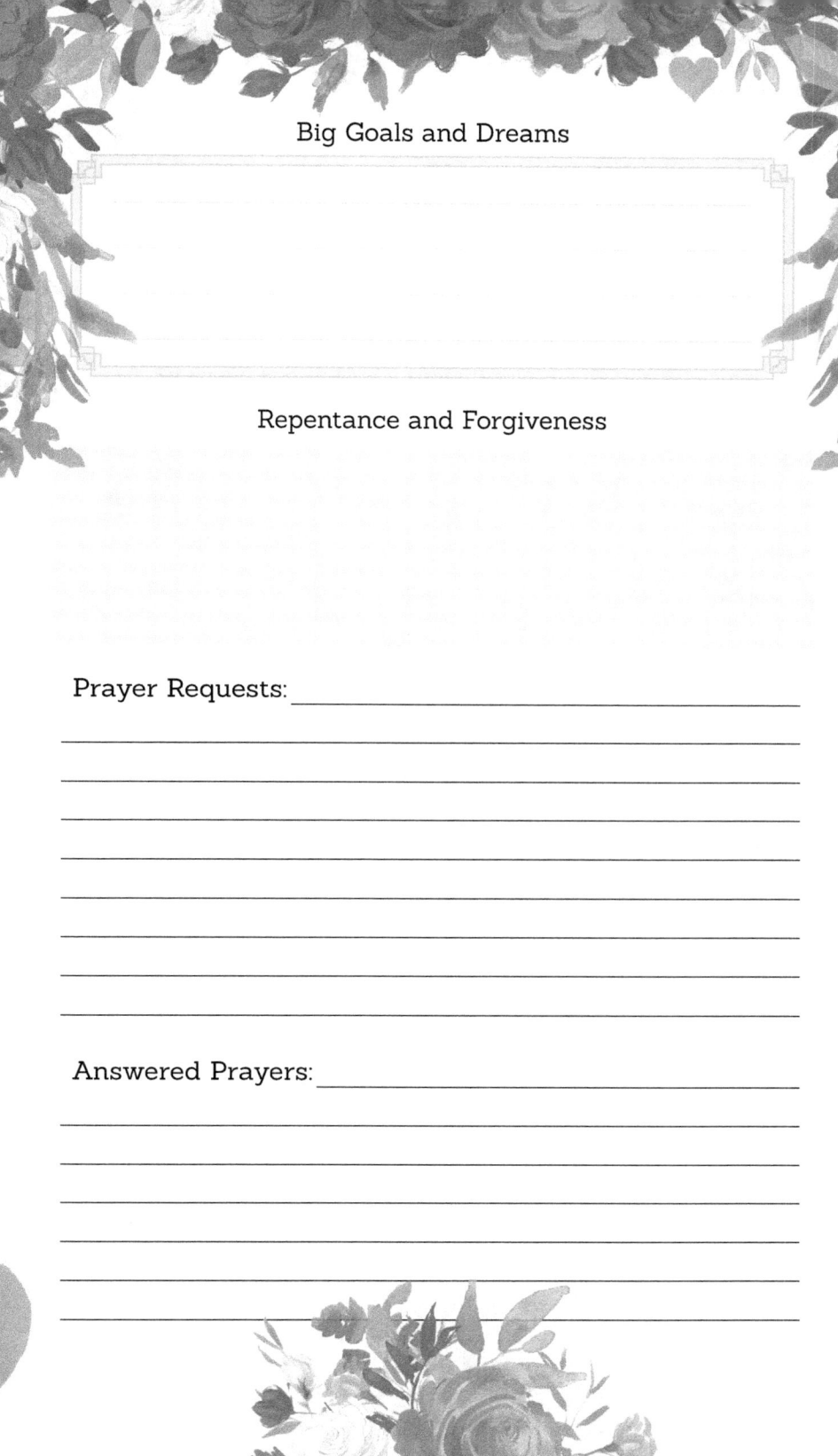

Big Goals and Dreams

Repentance and Forgiveness

Prayer Requests: _____

_____
_____
_____
_____
_____
_____
_____
_____
_____

Answered Prayers: _____

_____
_____
_____
_____
_____
_____

Brokenness Brings Wisdom

Date: _____

Bible Study, Meditation & Memory Verses

Gratitude & Praise to God: _____
_____
_____
_____
_____
_____
_____
_____

Brokenness Reflections

Big Goals and Dreams

Repentance and Forgiveness

Prayer Requests: _____
_____
_____
_____
_____
_____
_____
_____
_____

Answered Prayers: _____
_____
_____
_____
_____
_____

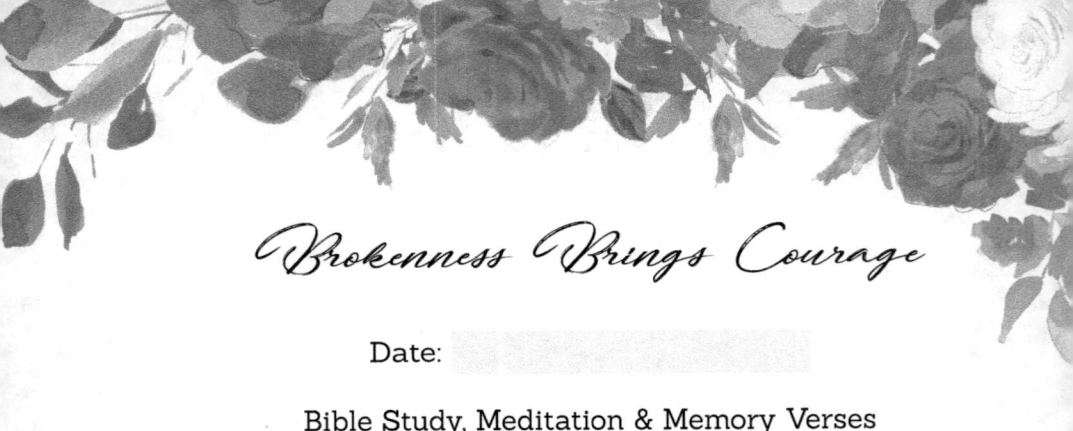

Brokenness Brings Courage

Date: _____

Bible Study, Meditation & Memory Verses

Gratitude & Praise to God: _____
_____
_____
_____
_____
_____
_____
_____
_____
_____

Brokenness Reflections

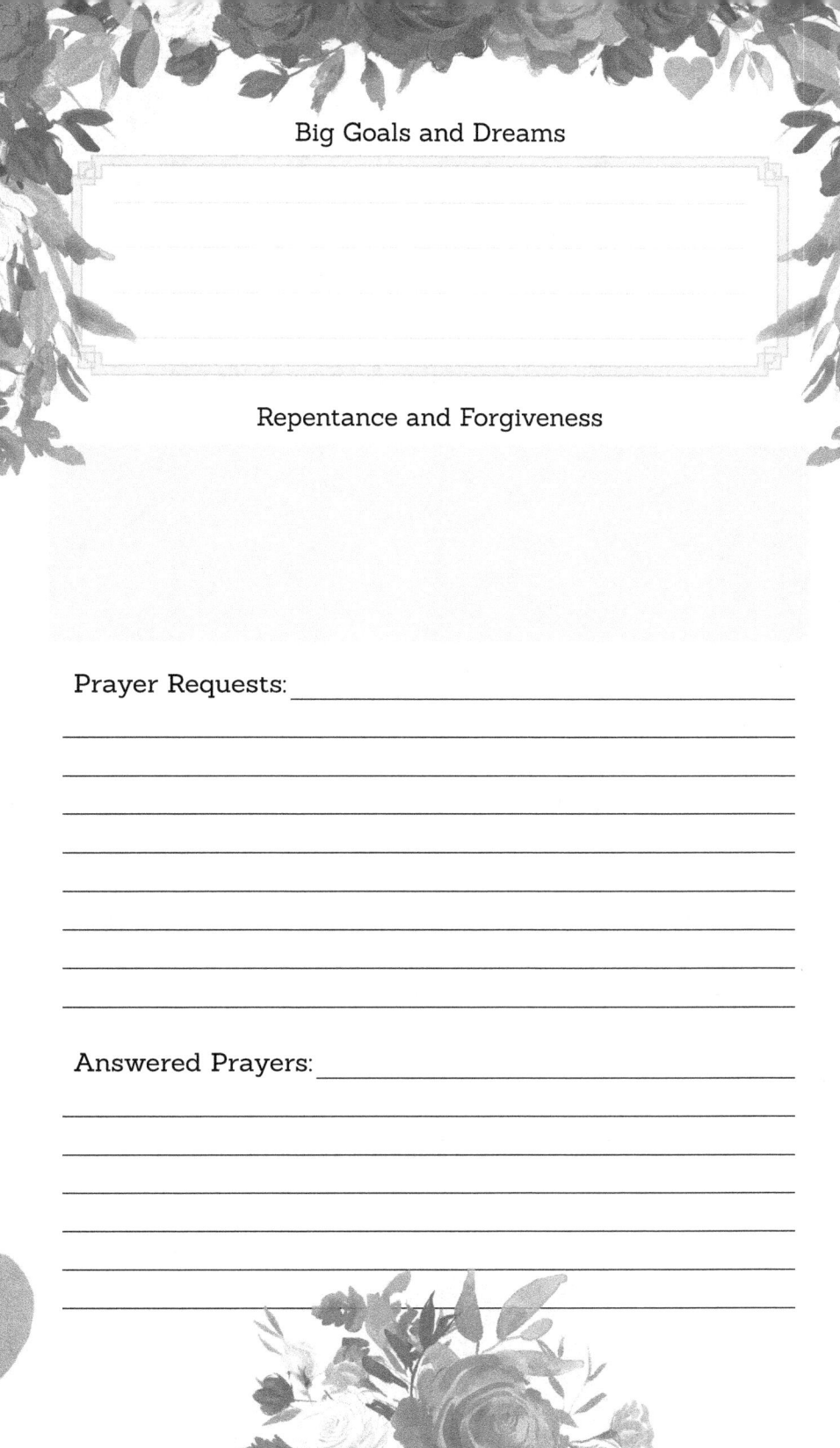

Big Goals and Dreams

Repentance and Forgiveness

Prayer Requests: _____
_____
_____
_____
_____
_____
_____
_____
_____
_____

Answered Prayers: _____
_____
_____
_____
_____
_____
_____

Brokenness Brings Self Control

Date: _____

Bible Study, Meditation & Memory Verses

Gratitude & Praise to God: _____
_____
_____
_____
_____
_____
_____
_____

Brokenness Reflections

Big Goals and Dreams

Repentance and Forgiveness

Prayer Requests: _____

_____
_____
_____
_____
_____
_____
_____
_____
_____

Answered Prayers: _____

_____
_____
_____
_____
_____
_____

Brokenness Brings Resilience

Date: _____

Bible Study, Meditation & Memory Verses

Gratitude & Praise to God: _____

_____
_____
_____
_____
_____
_____
_____

Brokenness Reflections

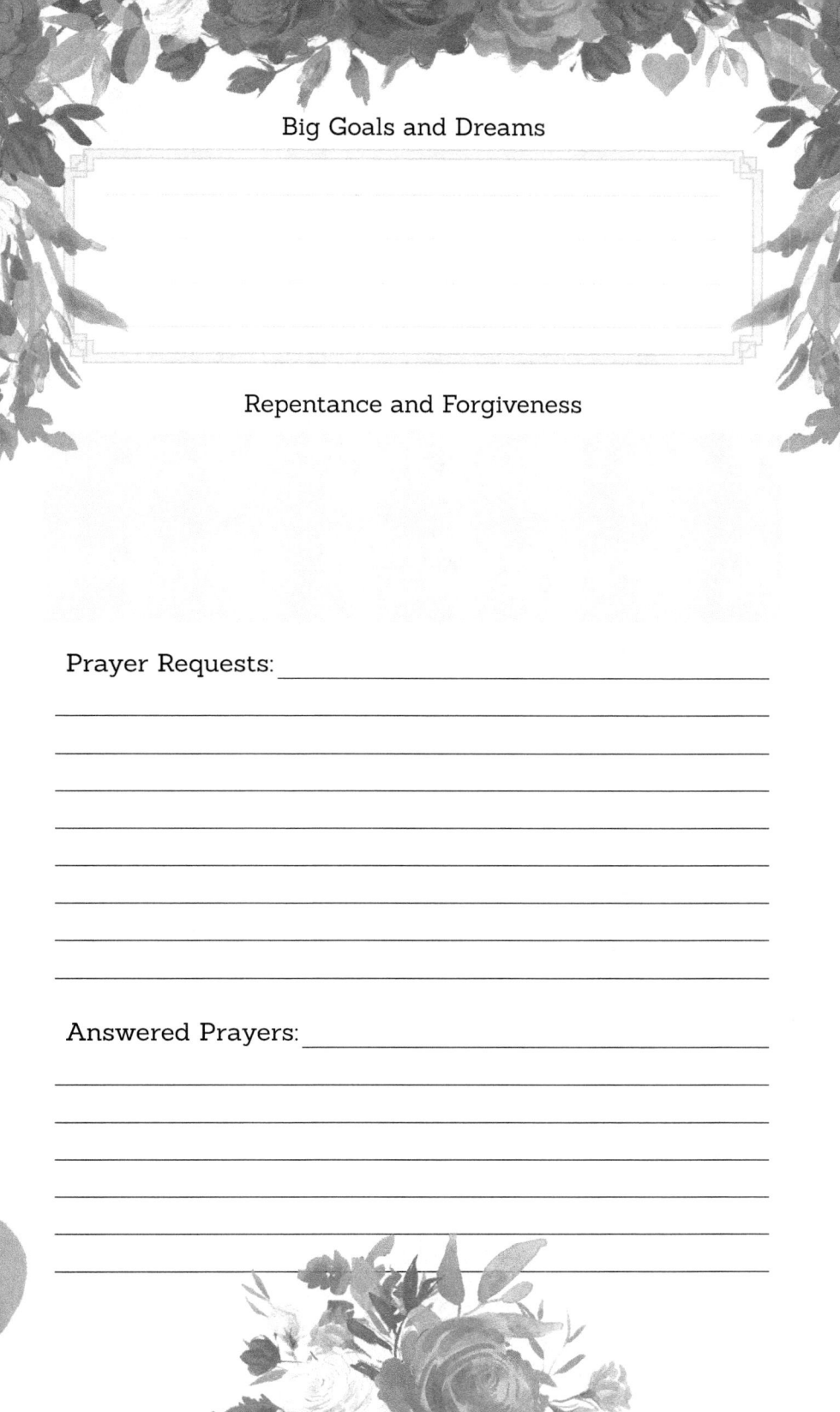

Big Goals and Dreams

Repentance and Forgiveness

Prayer Requests: _____

Answered Prayers: _____

Brokenness Brings Faith

Date: _____

Bible Study, Meditation & Memory Verses

Gratitude & Praise to God: _____
_____
_____
_____
_____
_____
_____
_____

Brokenness Reflections

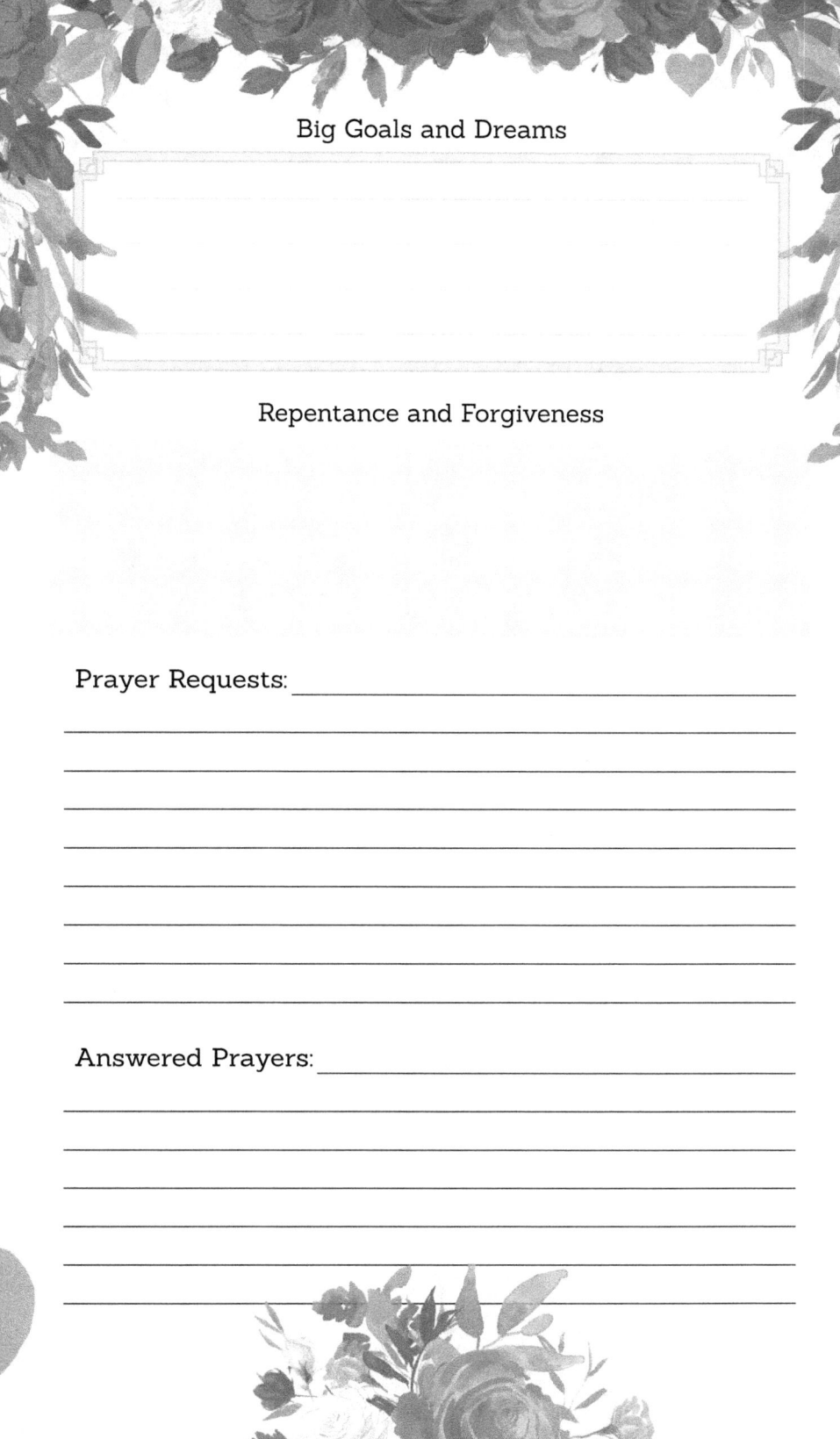

Big Goals and Dreams

Repentance and Forgiveness

Prayer Requests: _____
_____
_____
_____
_____
_____
_____
_____
_____
_____

Answered Prayers: _____
_____
_____
_____
_____
_____

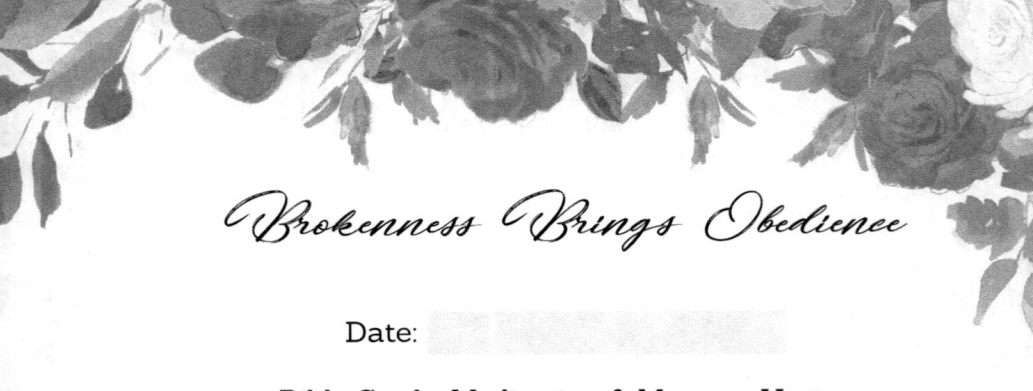

Brokenness Brings Obedience

Date: _____

Bible Study, Meditation & Memory Verses

Gratitude & Praise to God: _____
_____
_____
_____
_____
_____
_____
_____

Brokenness Reflections

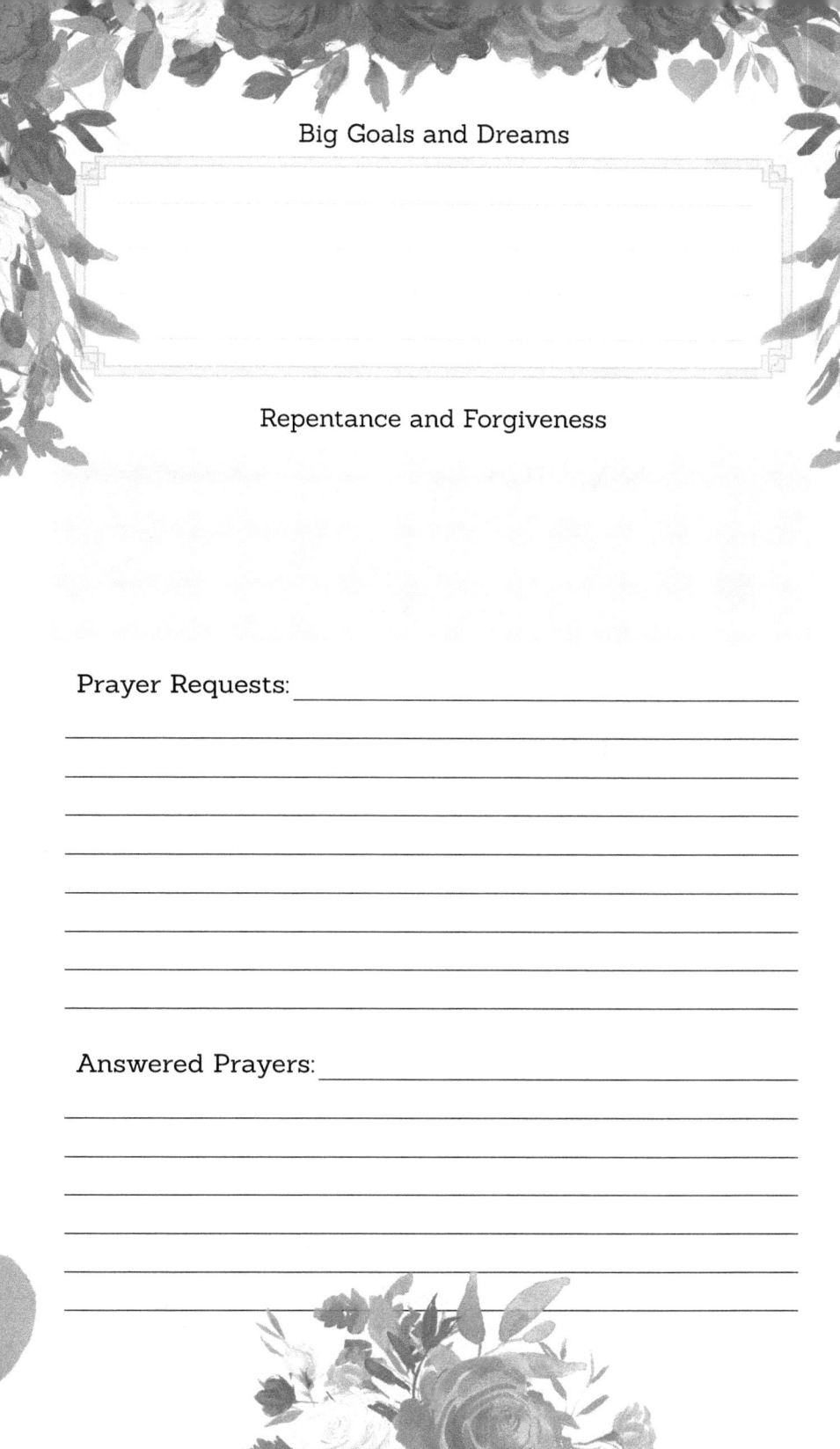

Big Goals and Dreams

Repentance and Forgiveness

Prayer Requests: _____
_____
_____
_____
_____
_____
_____
_____
_____
_____

Answered Prayers: _____
_____
_____
_____
_____
_____

Home Goal

Brokenness makes it easy to love others and receive love.

Start Date: _____   Achieve by: _____

Describe Your Home Goal

_____
_____
_____
_____

Progress Check

Actionable Steps

- ○ _____
- ○ _____
- ○ _____
- ○ _____
- ○ _____
- ○ _____

Reason for This Goal

_____
_____
_____
_____
_____

Challenges

Notes: _____
_____
_____
_____
_____
_____

Brokenness Brings Mercifulness

Date: _____

Bible Study, Meditation & Memory Verses

Gratitude & Praise to God: _____
_____
_____
_____
_____
_____
_____
_____

Brokenness Reflections

Big Goals and Dreams

Repentance and Forgiveness

Prayer Requests: _____
_____
_____
_____
_____
_____
_____
_____
_____
_____

Answered Prayers: _____
_____
_____
_____
_____
_____
_____
_____

Brokenness Brings Empathy

Date: _____

Bible Study, Meditation & Memory Verses

Gratitude & Praise to God: _____
_____
_____
_____
_____
_____
_____
_____
_____

Brokenness Reflections

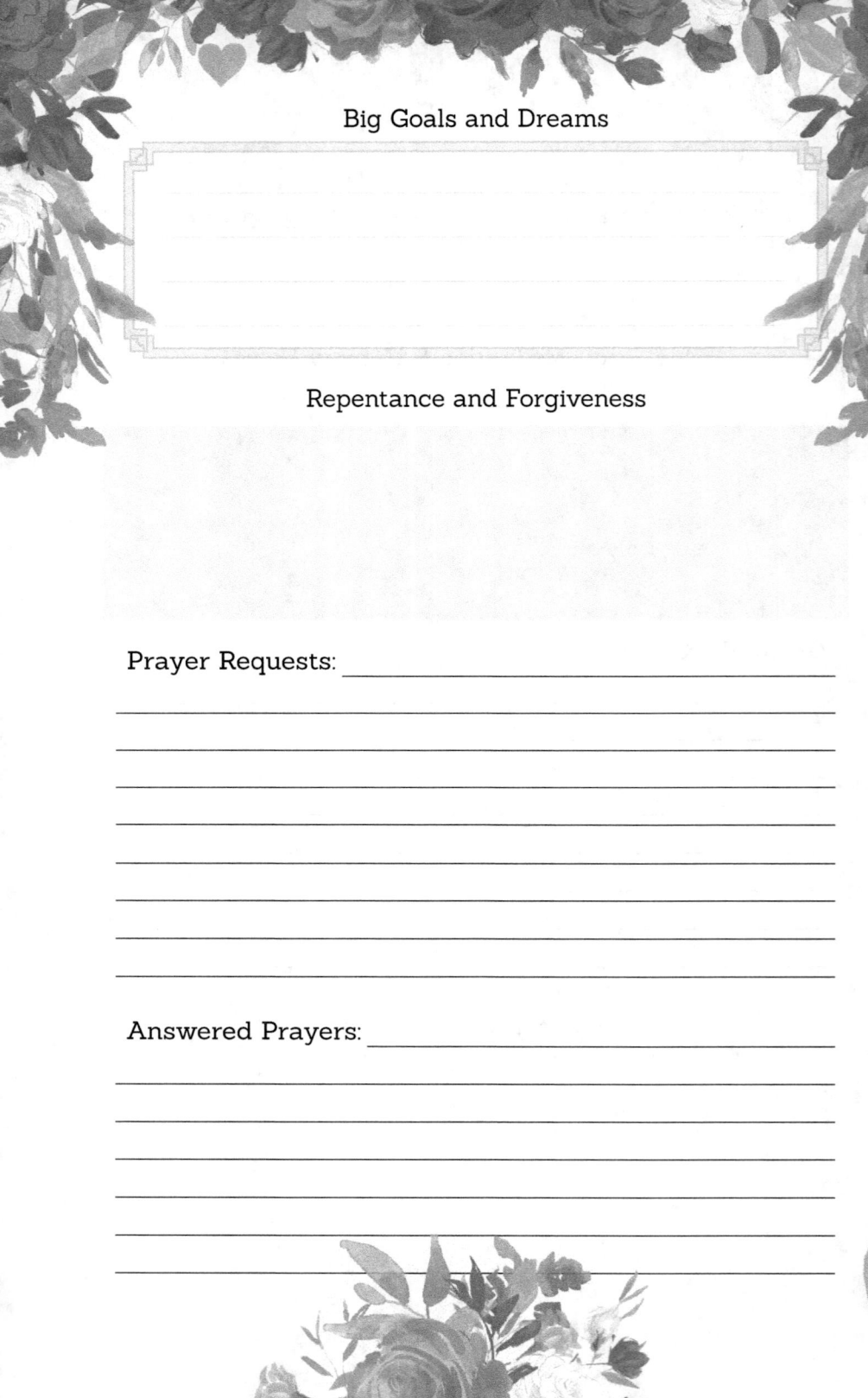

Big Goals and Dreams

Repentance and Forgiveness

Prayer Requests: _____

Answered Prayers: _____

Brokenness Brings a Loving Spirit

Date:

Bible Study, Meditation & Memory Verses

Gratitude & Praise to God: _____
_____
_____
_____
_____
_____
_____
_____
_____

Brokenness Reflections

Big Goals and Dreams

Repentance and Forgiveness

Prayer Requests: _____

_____
_____
_____
_____
_____
_____
_____
_____
_____

Answered Prayers: _____

_____
_____
_____
_____
_____
_____

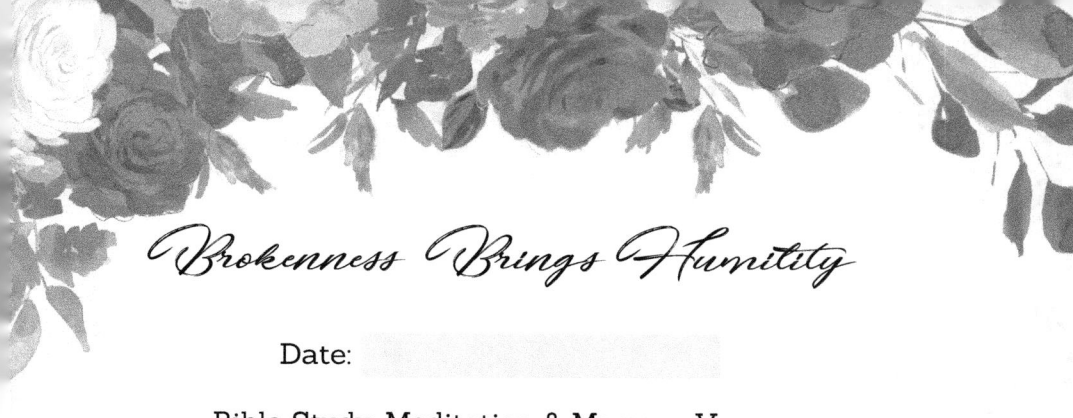

Brokenness Brings Humility

Date: _____

Bible Study, Meditation & Memory Verses

Gratitude & Praise to God: _____
_____
_____
_____
_____
_____
_____
_____
_____

Brokenness Reflections

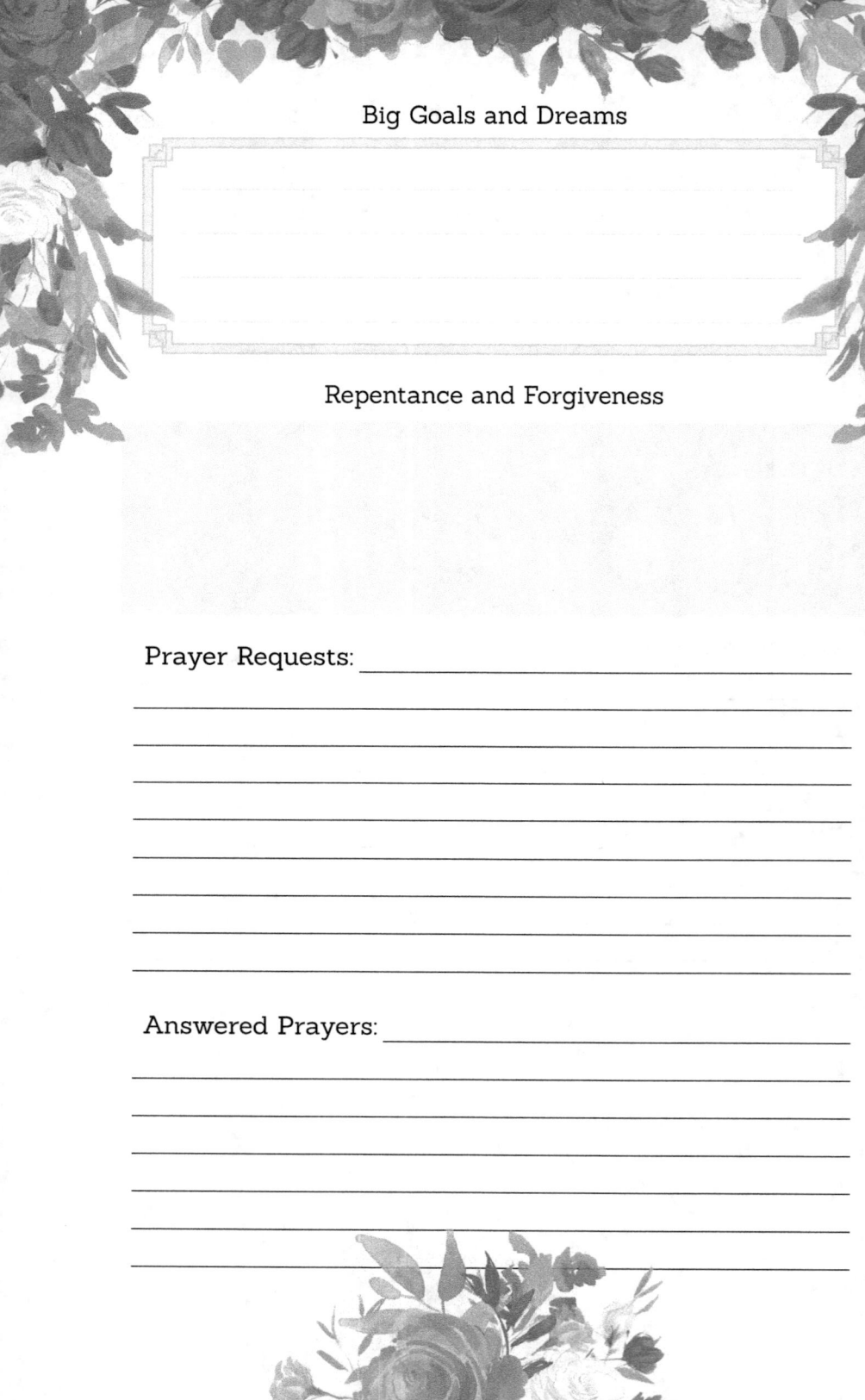

Big Goals and Dreams

Repentance and Forgiveness

Prayer Requests: _____

_____
_____
_____
_____
_____
_____
_____
_____
_____

Answered Prayers: _____

_____
_____
_____
_____
_____
_____
_____

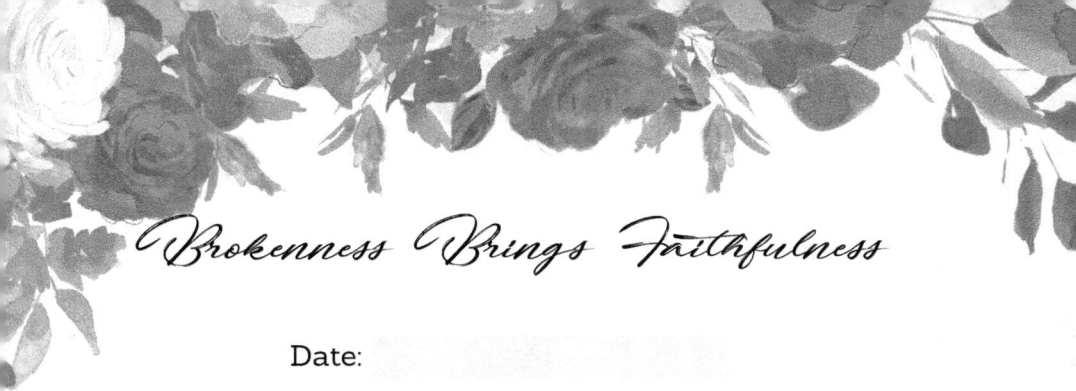

Brokenness Brings Faithfulness

Date: _____

Bible Study, Meditation & Memory Verses

Gratitude & Praise to God: _____
_____
_____
_____
_____
_____
_____
_____
_____
_____

Brokenness Reflections

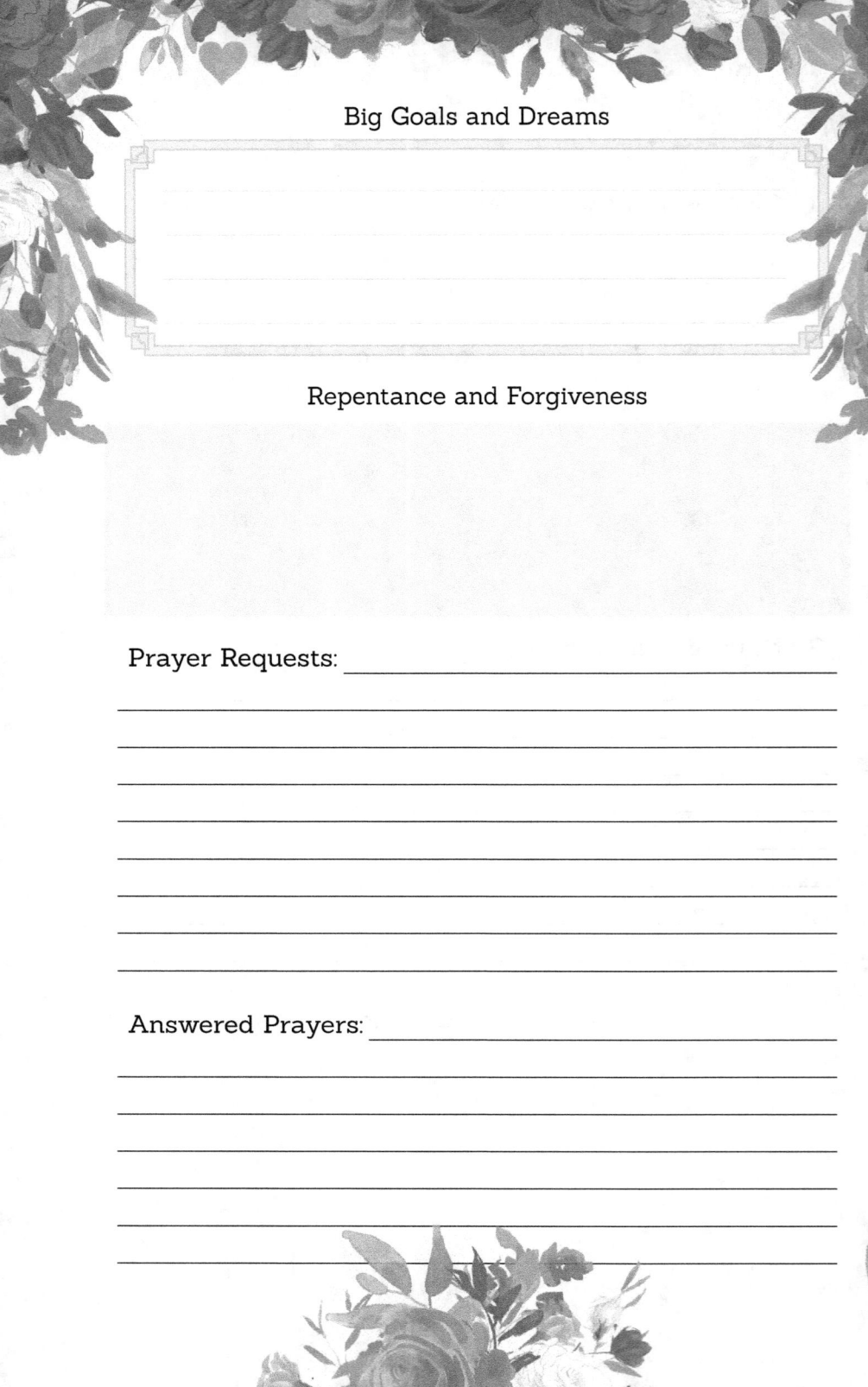

Big Goals and Dreams

Repentance and Forgiveness

Prayer Requests: _____

_____
_____
_____
_____
_____
_____
_____
_____
_____

Answered Prayers: _____

_____
_____
_____
_____
_____
_____
_____

Brokenness Brings Nurturing

Date: _____

Bible Study, Meditation & Memory Verses

Gratitude & Praise to God: _____
_____
_____
_____
_____
_____
_____
_____
_____

Brokenness Reflections

Big Goals and Dreams

Repentance and Forgiveness

Prayer Requests: _____
_____
_____
_____
_____
_____
_____
_____
_____
_____

Answered Prayers: _____
_____
_____
_____
_____
_____
_____
_____

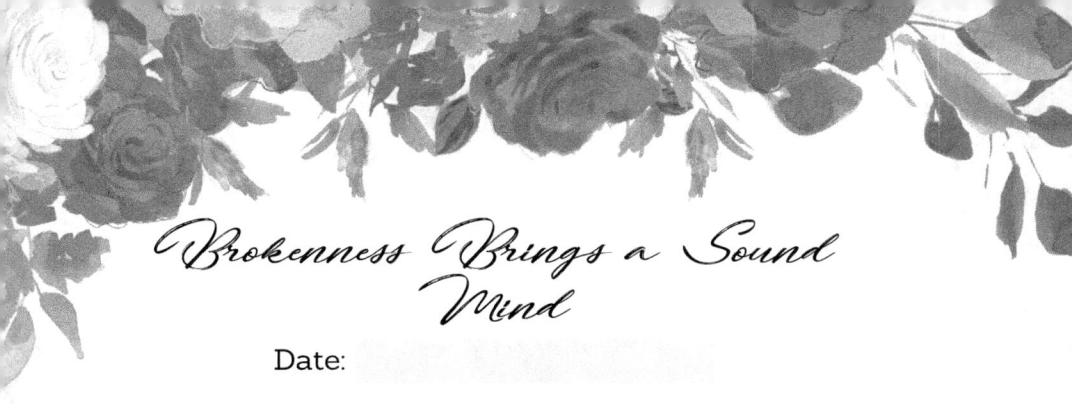

Brokenness Brings a Sound Mind

Date:

Bible Study, Meditation & Memory Verses

Gratitude & Praise to God: _____
_____
_____
_____
_____
_____
_____
_____

Brokenness Reflections

Big Goals and Dreams

Repentance and Forgiveness

Prayer Requests: _____
_____
_____
_____
_____
_____
_____
_____
_____

Answered Prayers: _____
_____
_____
_____
_____
_____
_____

Brokenness Brings Gratitude

Date: _____

Bible Study, Meditation & Memory Verses

Gratitude & Praise to God: _____
_____
_____
_____
_____
_____
_____
_____
_____

Brokenness Reflections

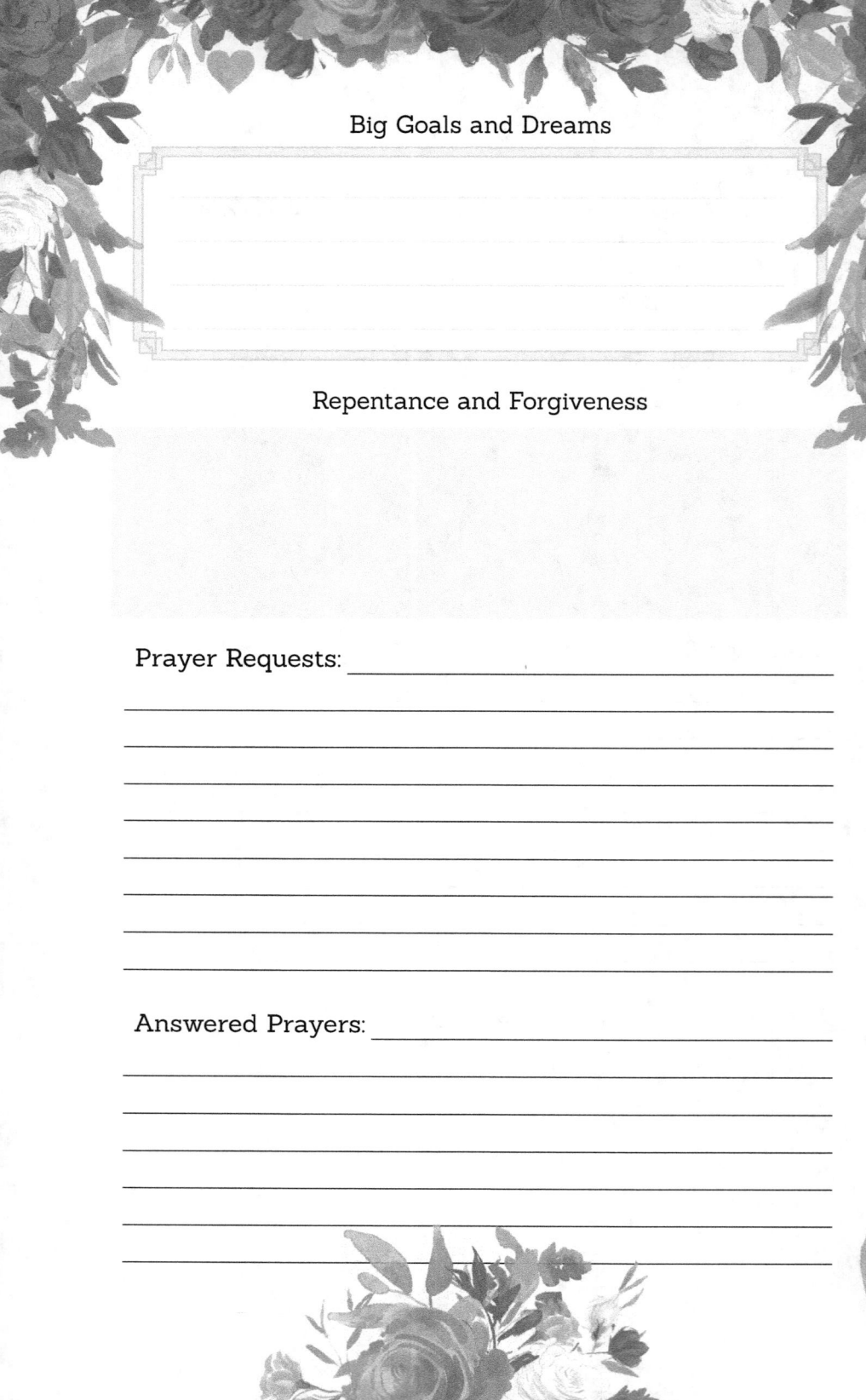

Big Goals and Dreams

Repentance and Forgiveness

Prayer Requests: _____
_____
_____
_____
_____
_____
_____
_____
_____

Answered Prayers: _____
_____
_____
_____
_____
_____
_____

Brokenness Brings Trust

Date:

Bible Study, Meditation & Memory Verses

Gratitude & Praise to God: _____
_____
_____
_____
_____
_____
_____
_____
_____

Brokenness Reflections

Big Goals and Dreams

Repentance and Forgiveness

Prayer Requests: _____
_____
_____
_____
_____
_____
_____
_____
_____
_____

Answered Prayers: _____
_____
_____
_____
_____
_____
_____

Brokenness Brings Generosity

Date: _____

Bible Study, Meditation & Memory Verses

Gratitude & Praise to God: _____
_____
_____
_____
_____
_____
_____
_____
_____

Brokenness Reflections

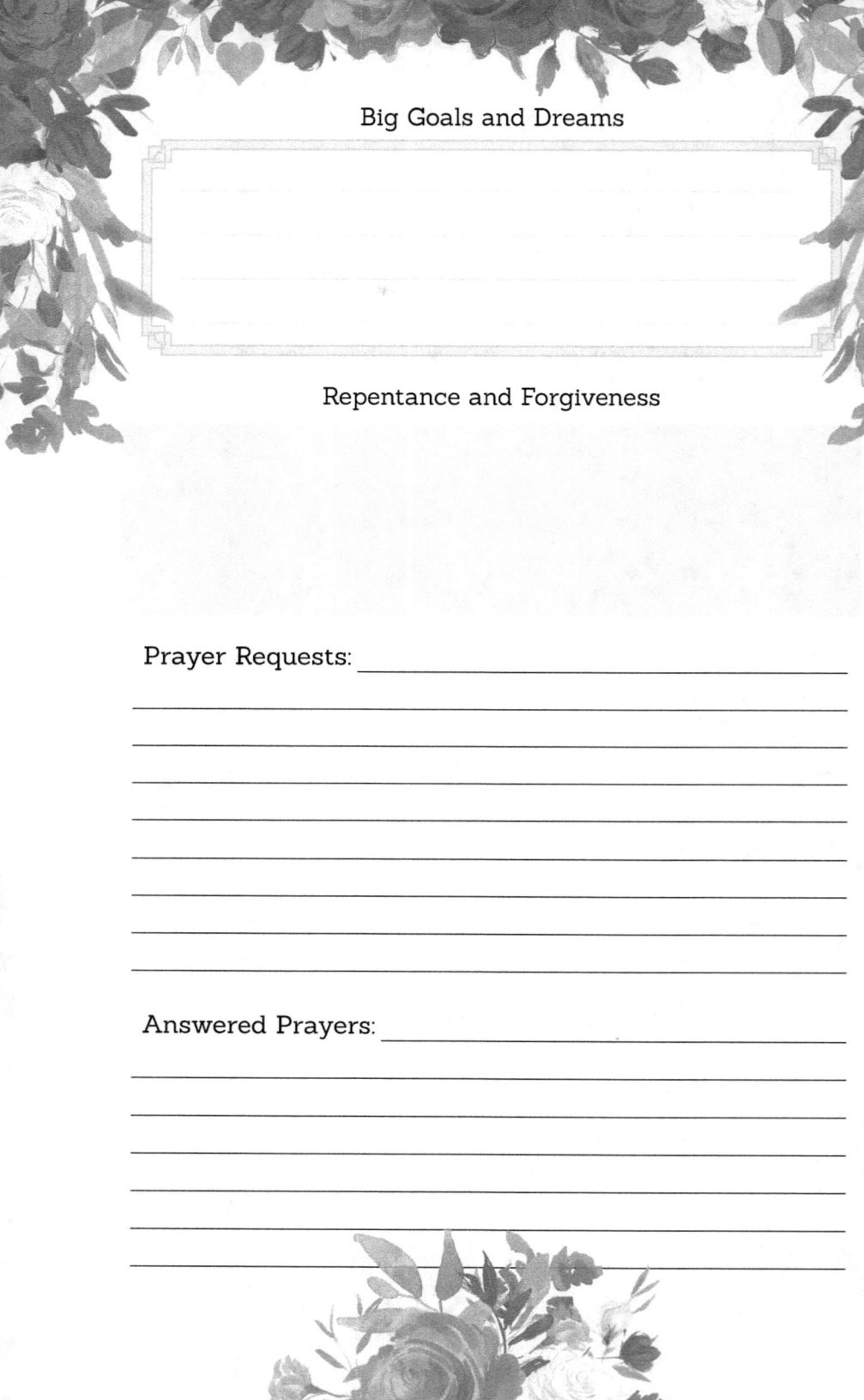

Big Goals and Dreams

Repentance and Forgiveness

Prayer Requests: _____

_____
_____
_____
_____
_____
_____
_____
_____
_____

Answered Prayers: _____

_____
_____
_____
_____
_____
_____

Health Goal

Brokenness cleans and refines us.

Start Date: Achieve by:

Describe Your Health Goal

Progress Check

Actionable Steps

-
-
-
-
-
-

Reason for This Goal

Challenges

Notes:

Brokenness Brings Integrity

Date: _____

Bible Study, Meditation & Memory Verses

Gratitude & Praise to God: _____
_____
_____
_____
_____
_____
_____
_____

Brokenness Reflections

Big Goals and Dreams

Repentance and Forgiveness

Prayer Requests: _____
_____
_____
_____
_____
_____
_____
_____
_____
_____

Answered Prayers: _____
_____
_____
_____
_____
_____
_____

Brokenness Brings Prayerfulness

Date:

Bible Study, Meditation & Memory Verses

Gratitude & Praise to God: _____

_____
_____
_____
_____
_____
_____
_____
_____

Brokenness Reflections

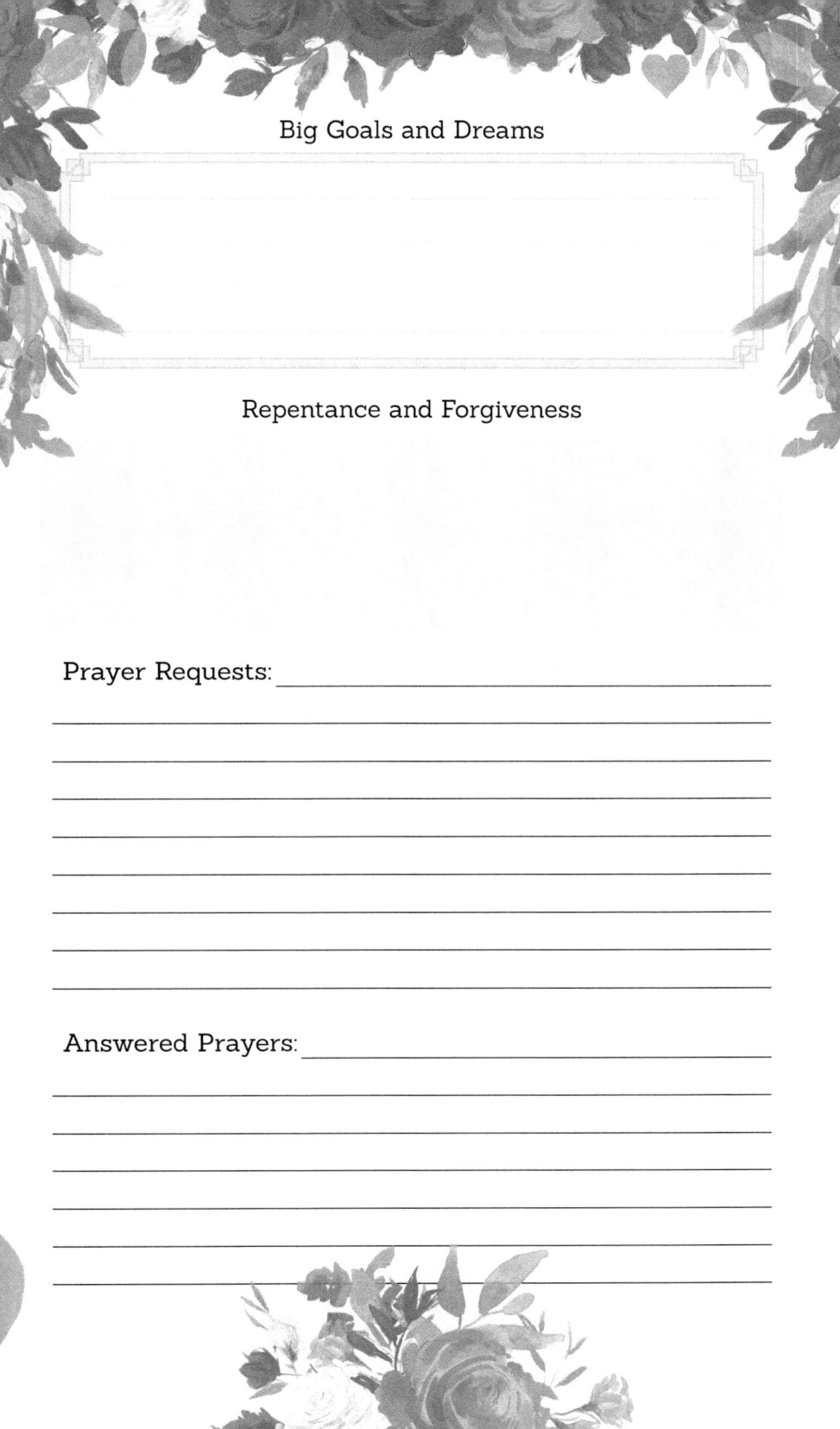

Big Goals and Dreams

Repentance and Forgiveness

Prayer Requests: _____
_____
_____
_____
_____
_____
_____
_____
_____
_____

Answered Prayers: _____
_____
_____
_____
_____
_____
_____

Brokenness Brings Righteousness

Date: _____

Bible Study, Meditation & Memory Verses

Gratitude & Praise to God: _____
_____
_____
_____
_____
_____
_____
_____
_____
_____

Brokenness Reflections

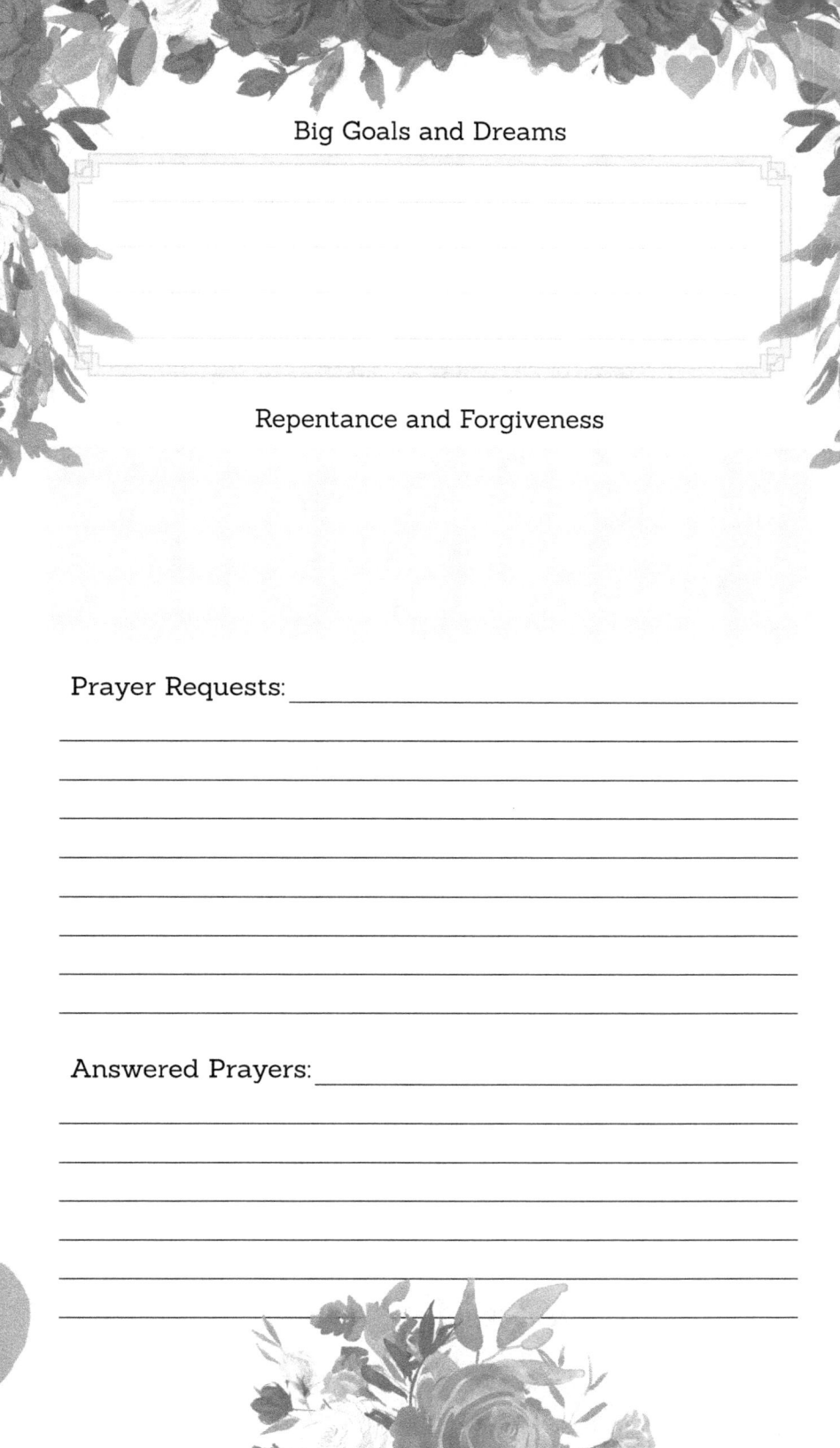

Big Goals and Dreams

Repentance and Forgiveness

Prayer Requests: _____
_____
_____
_____
_____
_____
_____
_____
_____
_____

Answered Prayers: _____
_____
_____
_____
_____
_____
_____

Brokenness Brings Honesty

Date: _____

Bible Study, Meditation & Memory Verses

Gratitude & Praise to God: _____
_____
_____
_____
_____
_____
_____
_____

Brokenness Reflections

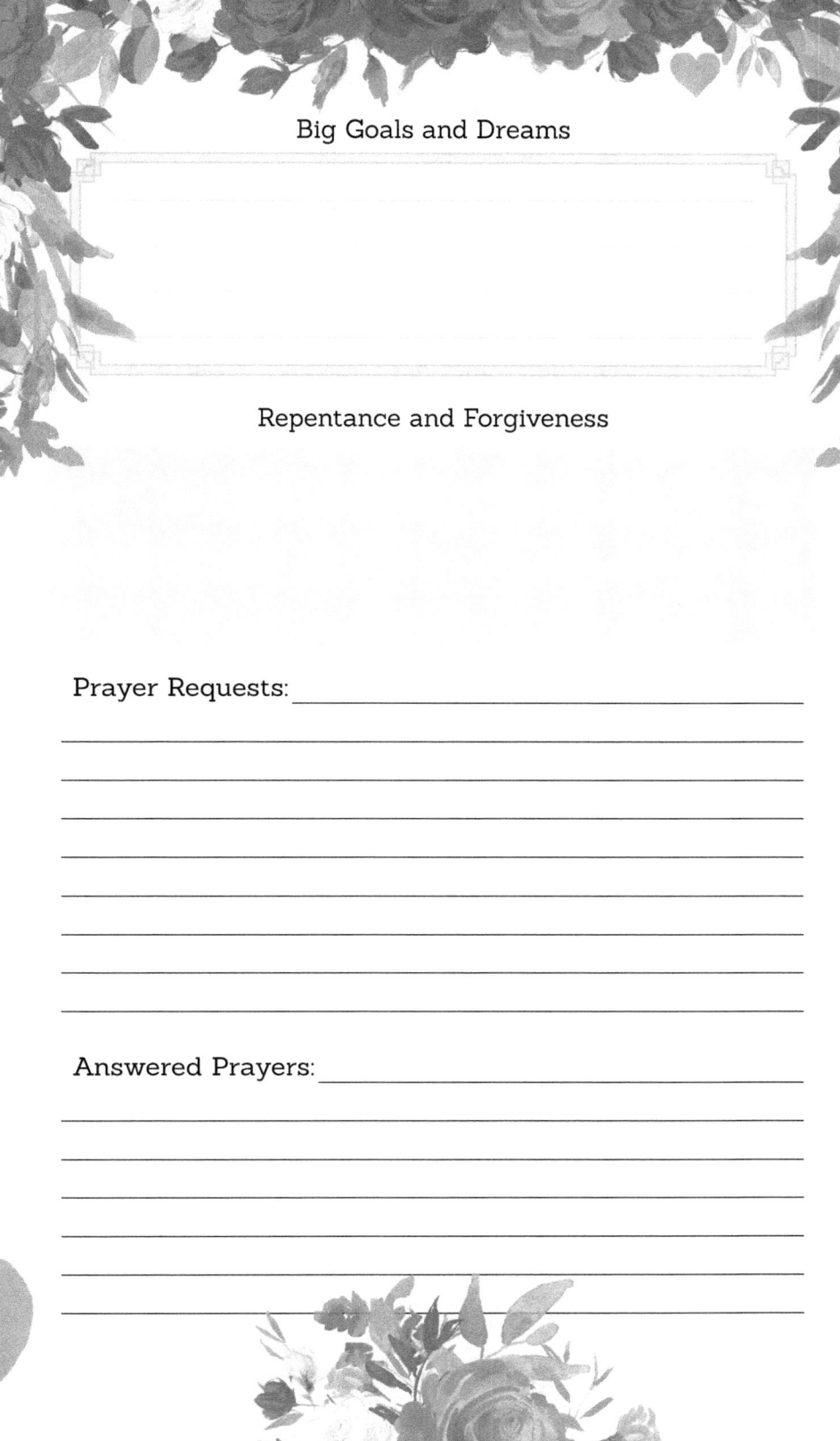

Big Goals and Dreams

Repentance and Forgiveness

Prayer Requests: _____
_____
_____
_____
_____
_____
_____
_____
_____
_____
_____

Answered Prayers: _____
_____
_____
_____
_____
_____
_____

Brokenness Brings Growth

Date: _____

Bible Study, Meditation & Memory Verses

Gratitude & Praise to God:

_____
_____
_____
_____
_____
_____
_____
_____

Brokenness Reflections

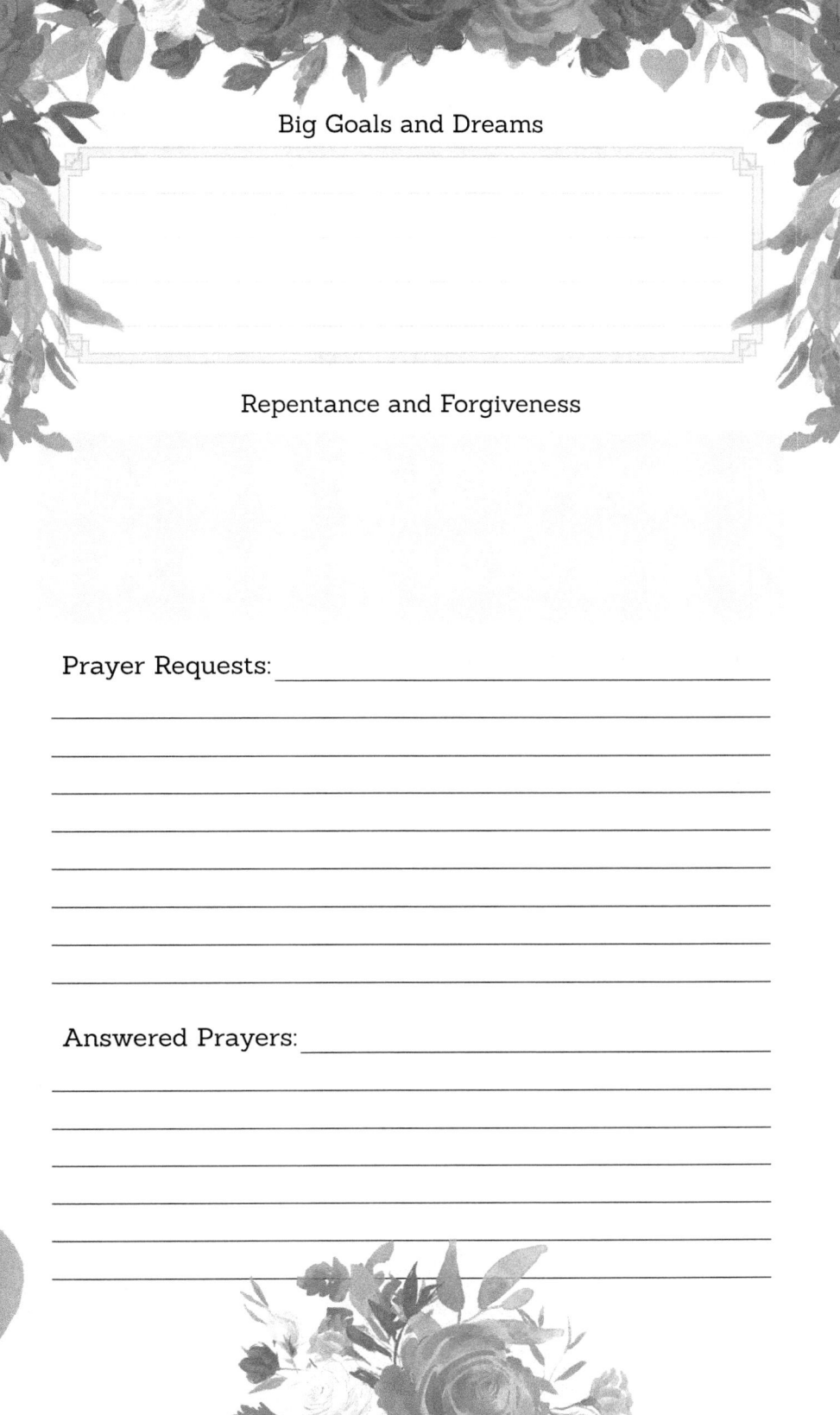

Big Goals and Dreams

Repentance and Forgiveness

Prayer Requests: _____

Answered Prayers: _____

Brokenness Brings Friendliness

Date: _____

Bible Study, Meditation & Memory Verses

Gratitude & Praise to God: _____
_____
_____
_____
_____
_____
_____
_____
_____
_____

Brokenness Reflections

Big Goals and Dreams

Repentance and Forgiveness

Prayer Requests: _____
_____
_____
_____
_____
_____
_____
_____
_____
_____
_____

Answered Prayers: _____
_____
_____
_____
_____
_____
_____

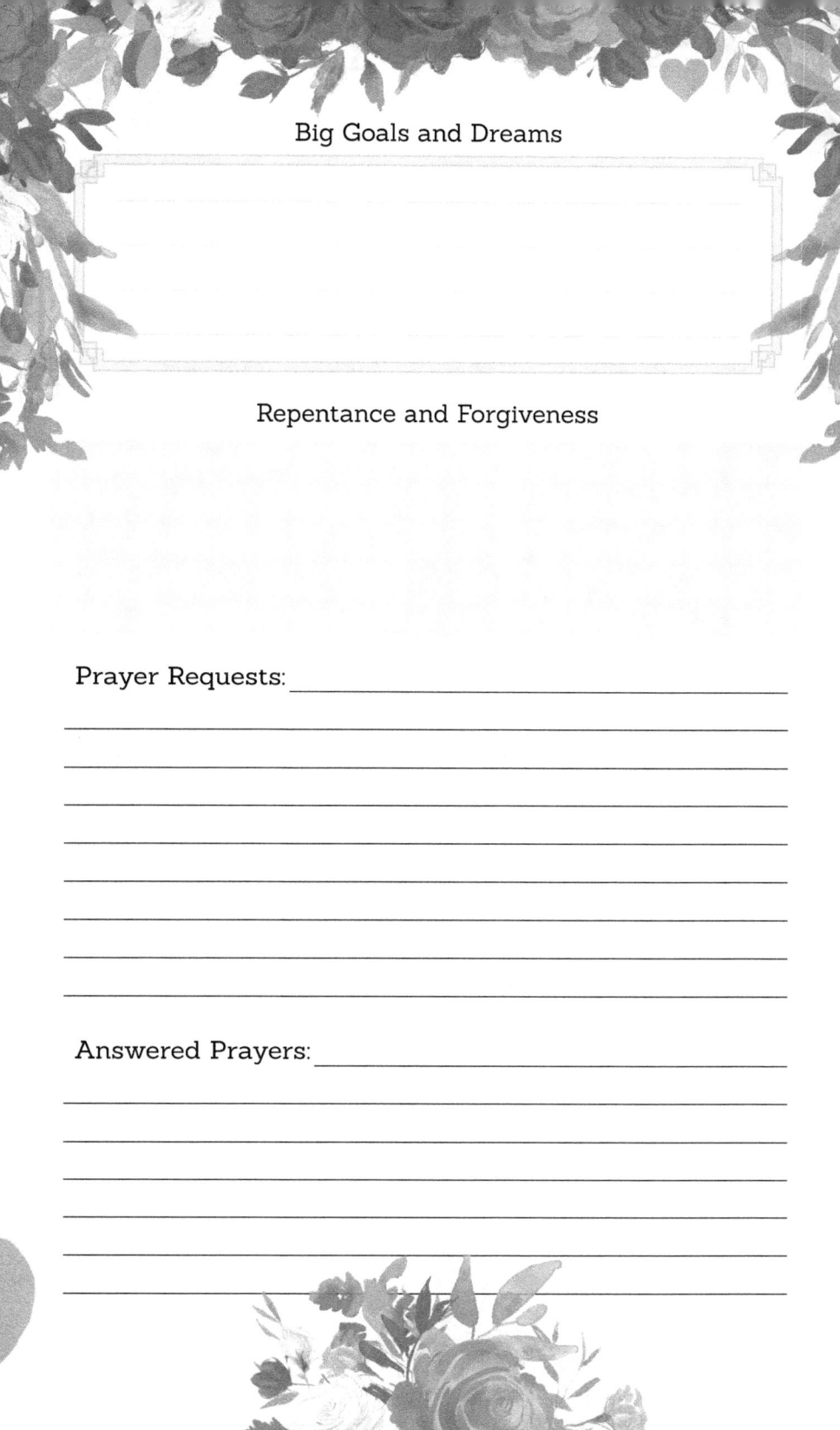

Brokenness Brings Confidence

Date: _____

Bible Study, Meditation & Memory Verses

Gratitude & Praise to God: _____
_____
_____
_____
_____
_____
_____
_____

Brokenness Reflections

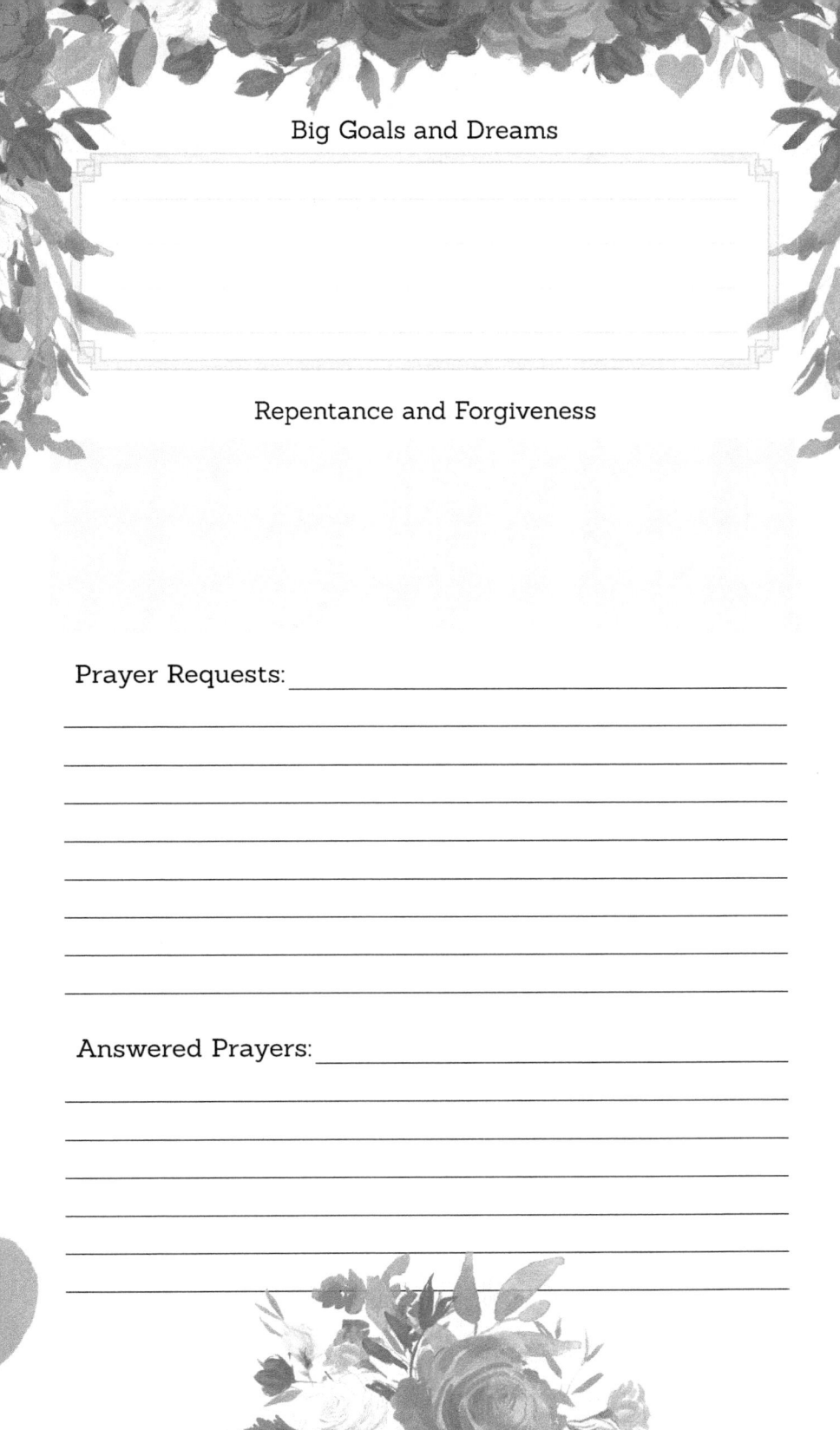

Big Goals and Dreams

Repentance and Forgiveness

Prayer Requests: _____

_____
_____
_____
_____
_____
_____
_____
_____
_____
_____

Answered Prayers: _____

_____
_____
_____
_____
_____
_____

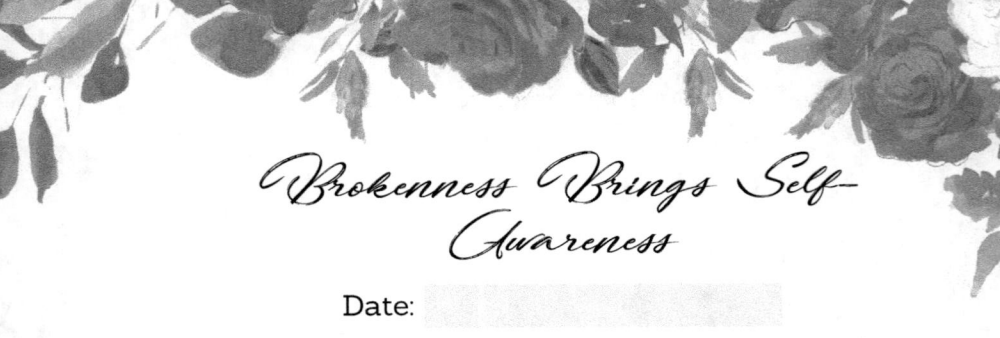

Brokenness Brings Self-Awareness

Date: _____

Bible Study, Meditation & Memory Verses

Gratitude & Praise to God: _____
_____
_____
_____
_____
_____
_____
_____

Brokenness Reflections

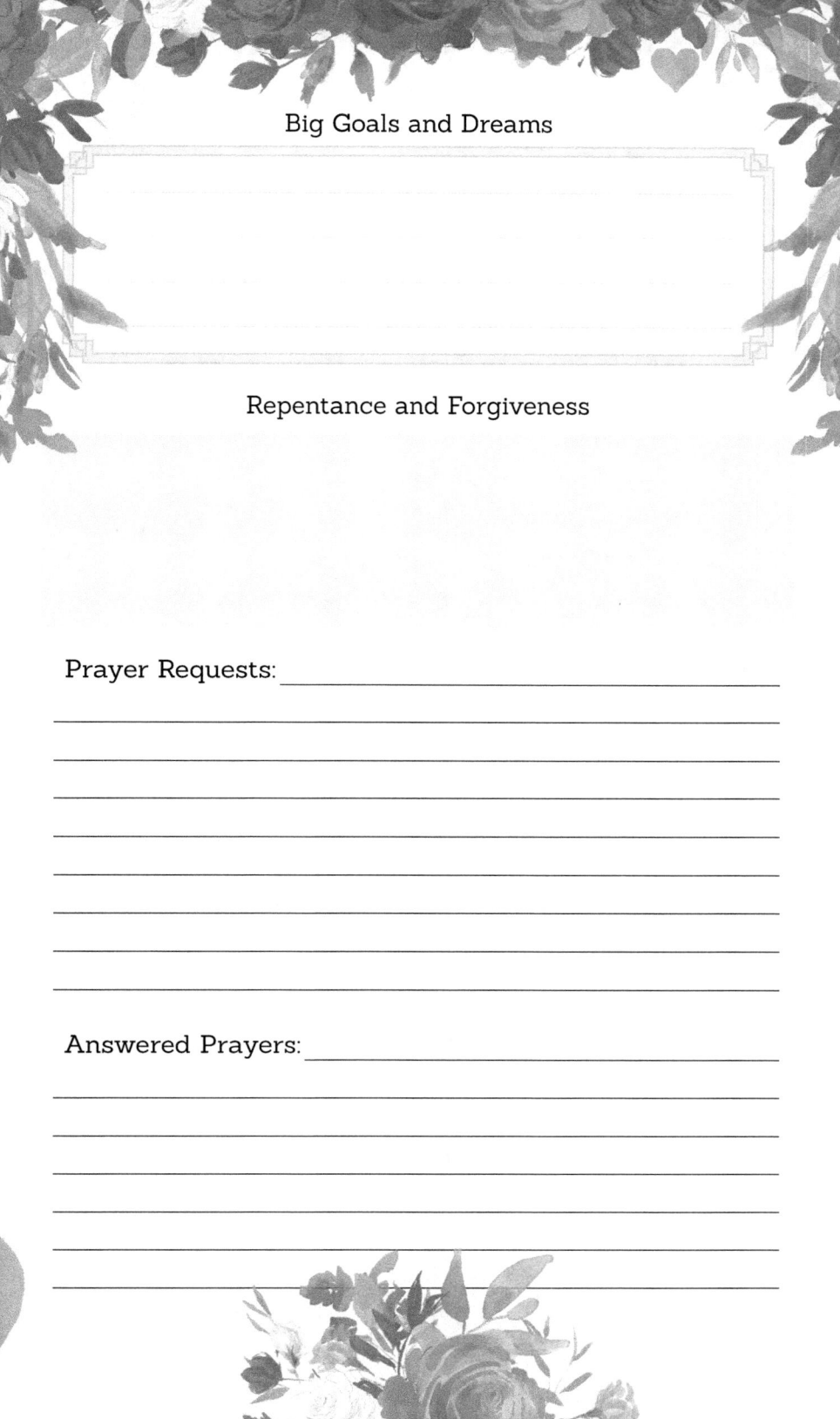

Big Goals and Dreams

Repentance and Forgiveness

Prayer Requests: _____

Answered Prayers: _____

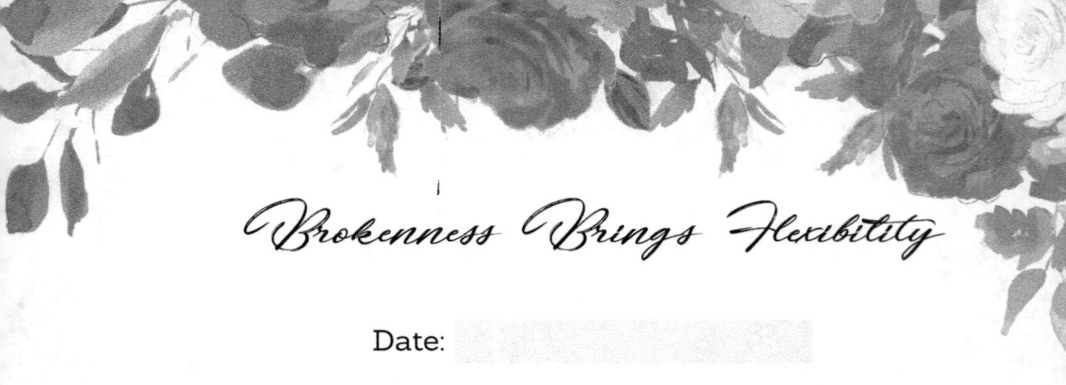

Brokenness Brings Flexibility

Date: _____

Bible Study, Meditation & Memory Verses

Gratitude & Praise to God: _____
_____
_____
_____
_____
_____
_____
_____
_____

Brokenness Reflections

Big Goals and Dreams

Repentance and Forgiveness

Prayer Requests: _____
_____
_____
_____
_____
_____
_____
_____
_____
_____

Answered Prayers: _____
_____
_____
_____
_____
_____
_____

Brokenness Brings Healing

Date: _____

Bible Study, Meditation & Memory Verses

Gratitude & Praise to God: _____

_____
_____
_____
_____
_____
_____
_____

Brokenness Reflections

Big Goals and Dreams

Repentance and Forgiveness

Prayer Requests: _____

_____
_____
_____
_____
_____
_____
_____
_____
_____

Answered Prayers: _____

_____
_____
_____
_____
_____

Career Goal

Brokenness breaks our stubbornness so that our full potential can be unleashed.

Start Date: _____   Achieve by: _____

Describe Your Career Goal

Progress Check

Actionable Steps

- ○
- ○
- ○
- ○
- ○
- ○

Reason for This Goal

Challenges

Notes:

Brokenness Brings Miracles

Date:

Bible Study, Meditation & Memory Verses

Gratitude & Praise to God: _____
_____
_____
_____
_____
_____
_____
_____
_____

Brokenness Reflections

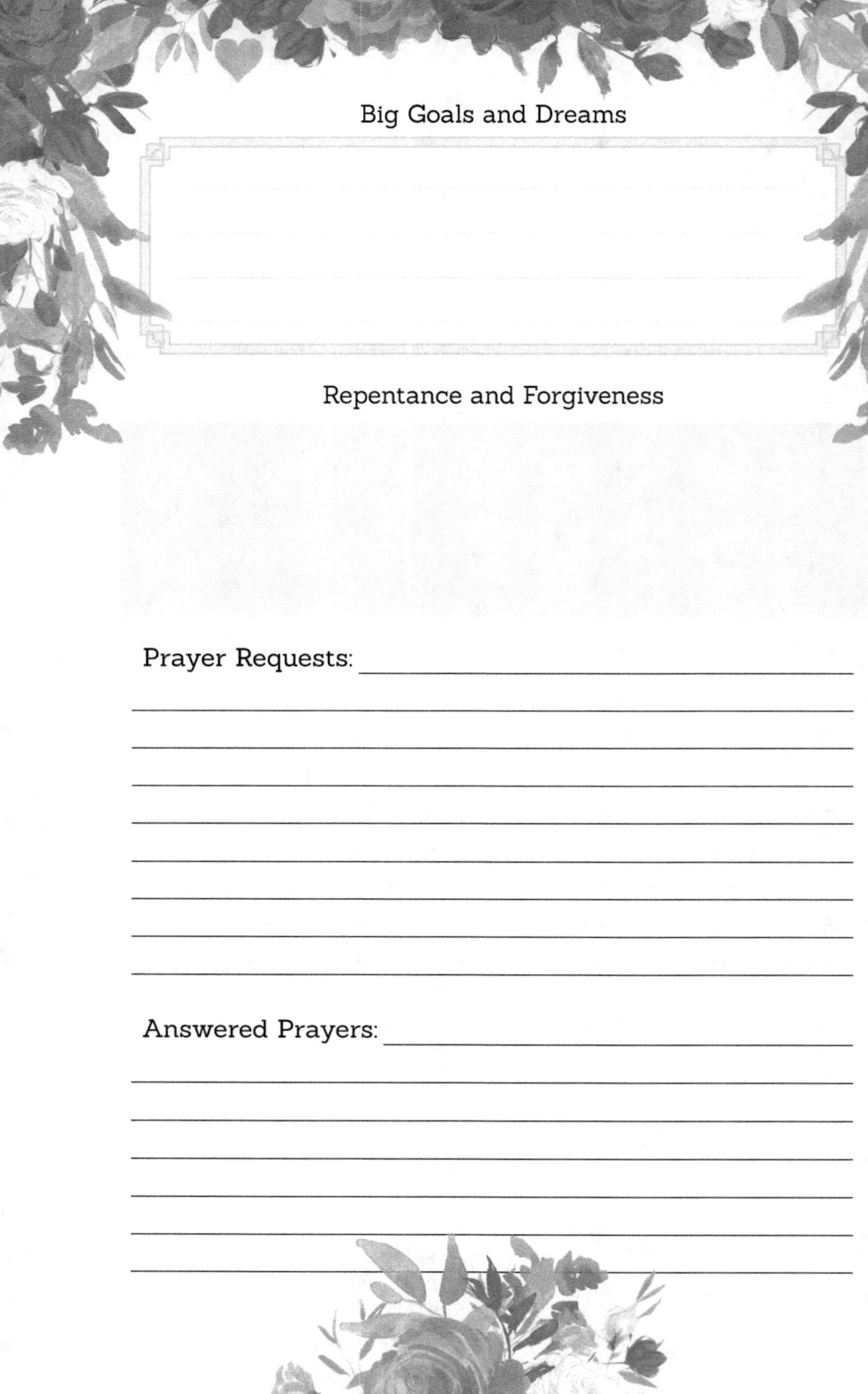

Big Goals and Dreams

Repentance and Forgiveness

Prayer Requests: _____

Answered Prayers: _____

Brokenness Brings Inner Beauty

Date:

Bible Study, Meditation & Memory Verses

Gratitude & Praise to God: _____
_____
_____
_____
_____
_____
_____
_____

Brokenness Reflections

Big Goals and Dreams

Repentance and Forgiveness

Prayer Requests: _____

_____
_____
_____
_____
_____
_____
_____
_____
_____

Answered Prayers: _____

_____
_____
_____
_____
_____
_____

Brokenness Brings Thankfulness

Date:

Bible Study, Meditation & Memory Verses

Gratitude & Praise to God: _____
_____
_____
_____
_____
_____
_____
_____
_____

Brokenness Reflections

Big Goals and Dreams

Repentance and Forgiveness

Prayer Requests: _____
_____
_____
_____
_____
_____
_____
_____
_____
_____

Answered Prayers: _____
_____
_____
_____
_____
_____
_____

Brokenness Brings Diligence

Date:

Bible Study, Meditation & Memory Verses

Gratitude & Praise to God: _____
_____
_____
_____
_____
_____
_____
_____

Brokenness Reflections

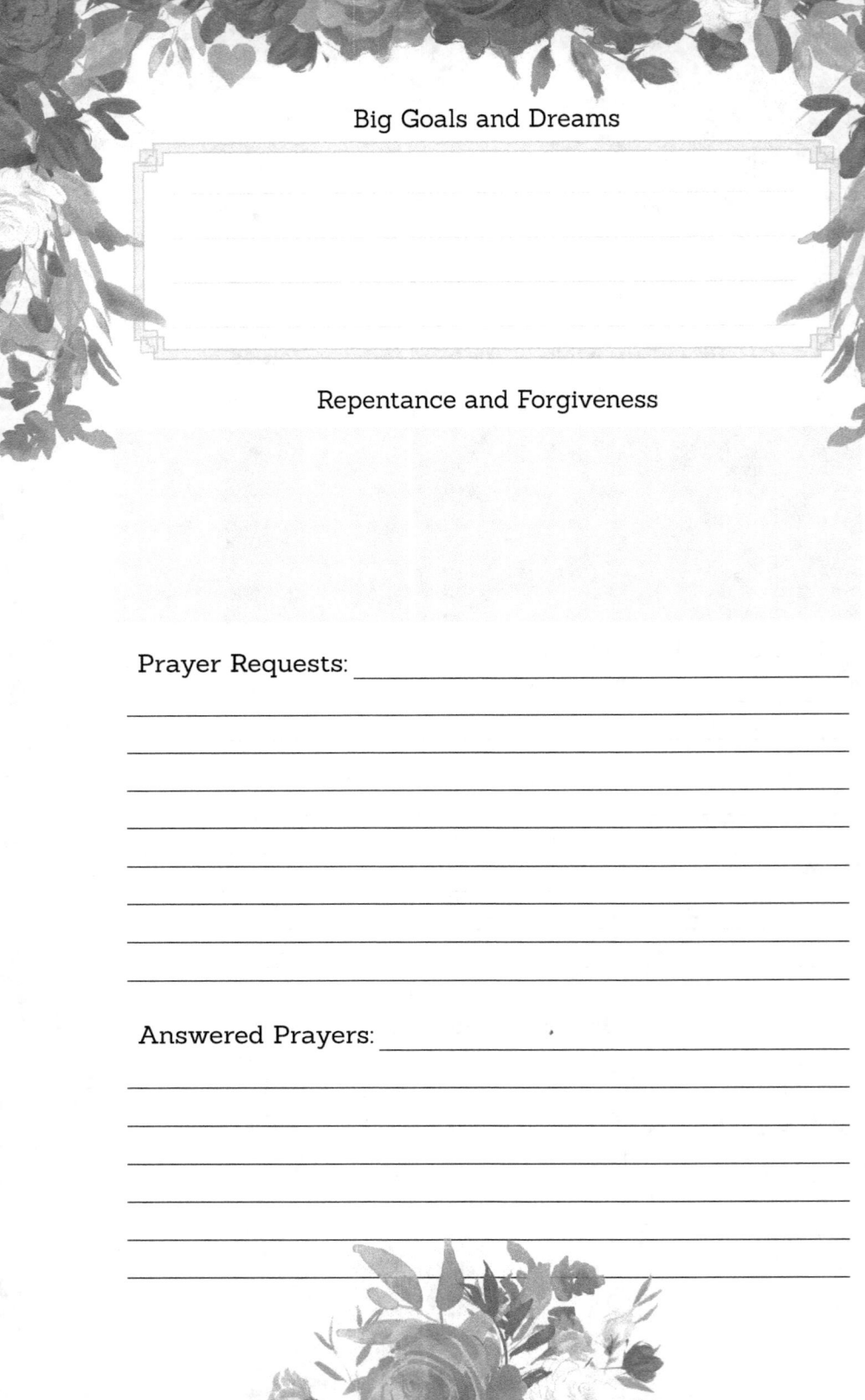

Big Goals and Dreams

Repentance and Forgiveness

Prayer Requests: _____

Answered Prayers: _____

Brokenness Brings Excellence

Date: _____

Bible Study, Meditation & Memory Verses

Gratitude & Praise to God: _____
_____
_____
_____
_____
_____
_____
_____
_____

Brokenness Reflections

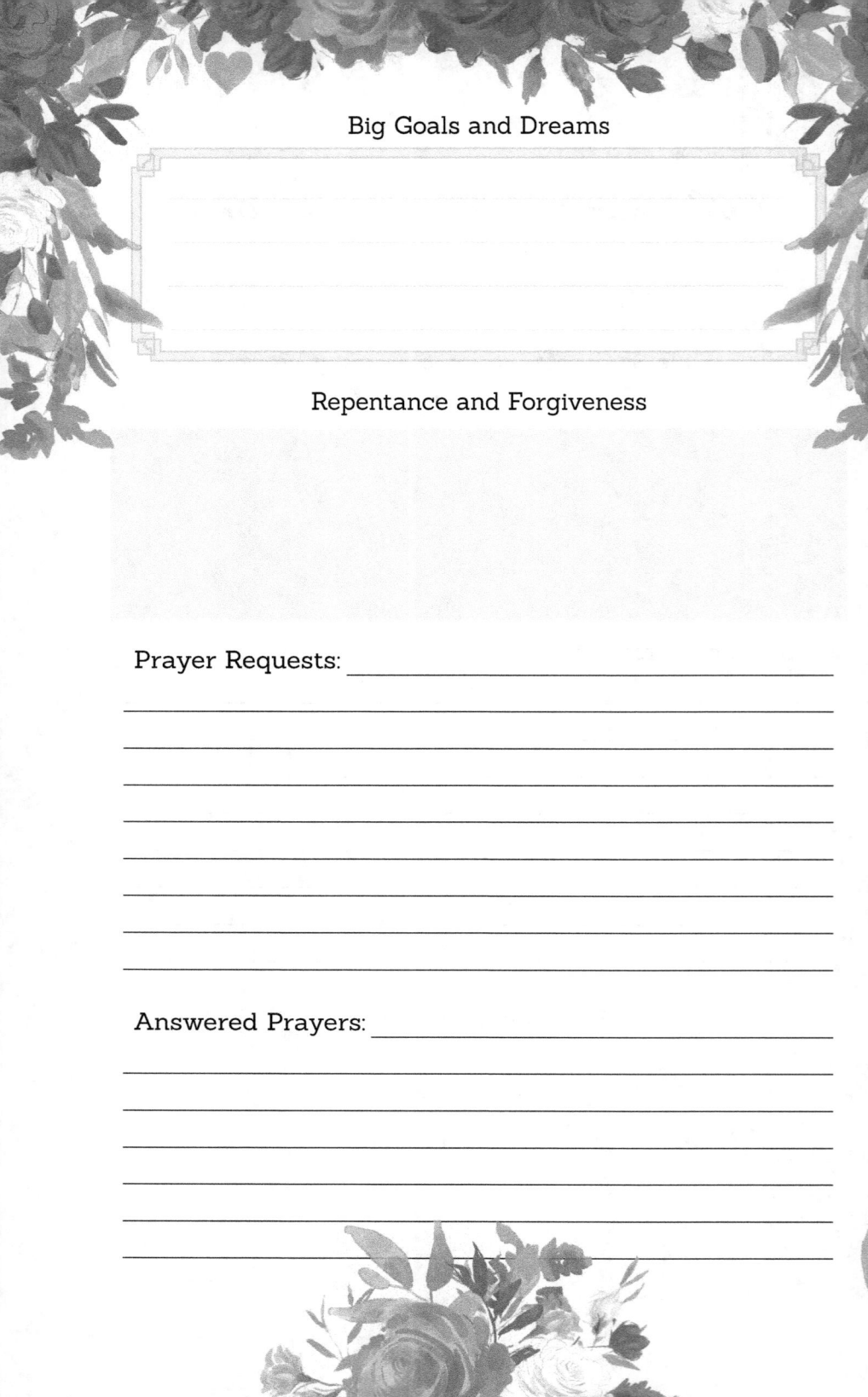

Big Goals and Dreams

Repentance and Forgiveness

Prayer Requests: _____
_____
_____
_____
_____
_____
_____
_____
_____

Answered Prayers: _____
_____
_____
_____
_____
_____
_____

Brokenness Brings Inspiration

Date:

Bible Study, Meditation & Memory Verses

Gratitude & Praise to God: _____
_____
_____
_____
_____
_____
_____
_____
_____
_____

Brokenness Reflections

Big Goals and Dreams

Repentance and Forgiveness

Prayer Requests: _____
_____
_____
_____
_____
_____
_____
_____
_____
_____

Answered Prayers: _____
_____
_____
_____
_____
_____
_____

Brokenness Brings Godly Character

Date:

Bible Study, Meditation & Memory Verses

Gratitude & Praise to God: _____
_____
_____
_____
_____
_____
_____
_____
_____

Brokenness Reflections

Big Goals and Dreams

Repentance and Forgiveness

Prayer Requests: _____
_____
_____
_____
_____
_____
_____
_____
_____
_____

Answered Prayers: _____
_____
_____
_____
_____
_____
_____

Brokenness Brings Protection

Date:

Bible Study, Meditation & Memory Verses

Gratitude & Praise to God: _____
_____
_____
_____
_____
_____
_____
_____

Brokenness Reflections

Big Goals and Dreams

Repentance and Forgiveness

Prayer Requests: _____

_____
_____
_____
_____
_____
_____
_____
_____

Answered Prayers: _____

_____
_____
_____
_____
_____
_____
_____

Brokenness Brings Discernment

Date:

Bible Study, Meditation & Memory Verses

Gratitude & Praise to God: _____

_____
_____
_____
_____
_____
_____
_____
_____

Brokenness Reflections

Big Goals and Dreams

Repentance and Forgiveness

Prayer Requests: _____
_____
_____
_____
_____
_____
_____
_____
_____
_____

Answered Prayers: _____
_____
_____
_____
_____
_____
_____
_____

Brokenness Brings Wholeness

Date:

Bible Study, Meditation & Memory Verses

Gratitude & Praise to God: _____
_____
_____
_____
_____
_____
_____
_____

Brokenness Reflections

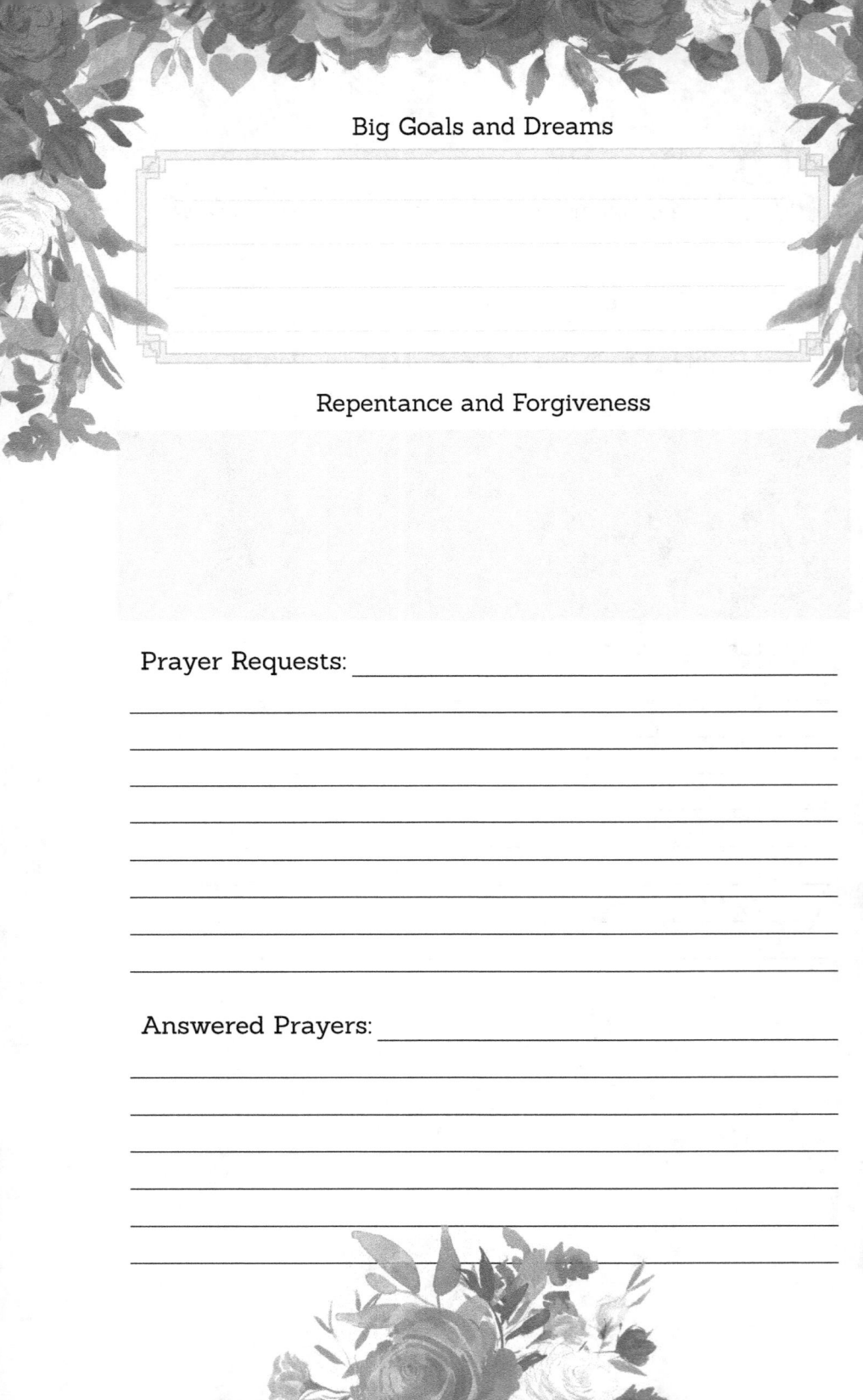

Big Goals and Dreams

Repentance and Forgiveness

Prayer Requests: _____

Answered Prayers: _____

Financial Goal

Brokenness is a gateway to incredible blessings.

Start Date: Achieve by:

Describe Your Financial Goal

_____
_____
_____
_____

Progress Check

Actionable Steps

- ○
- ○
- ○
- ○
- ○
- ○

Reason for This Goal

_____
_____
_____
_____
_____

Challenges

Notes: _____
_____
_____
_____
_____
_____
_____

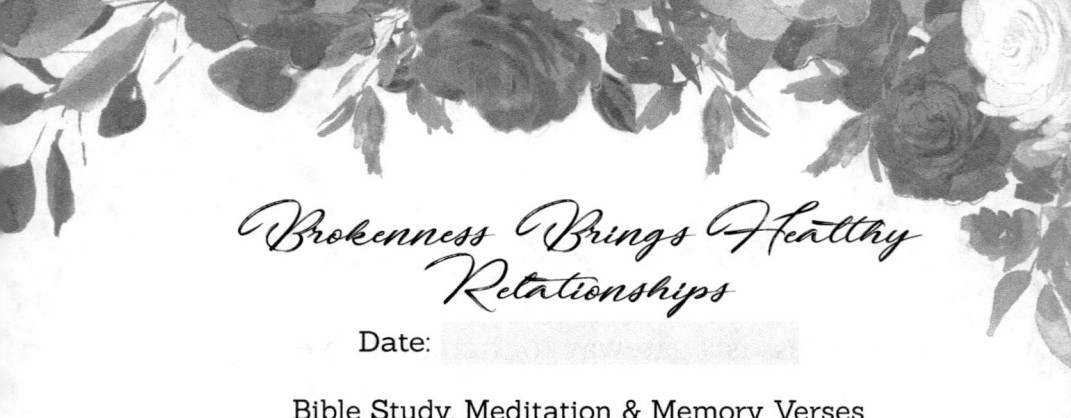

Brokenness Brings Healthy Relationships

Date: _____

Bible Study, Meditation & Memory Verses

Gratitude & Praise to God: _____
_____
_____
_____
_____
_____
_____
_____

Brokenness Reflections

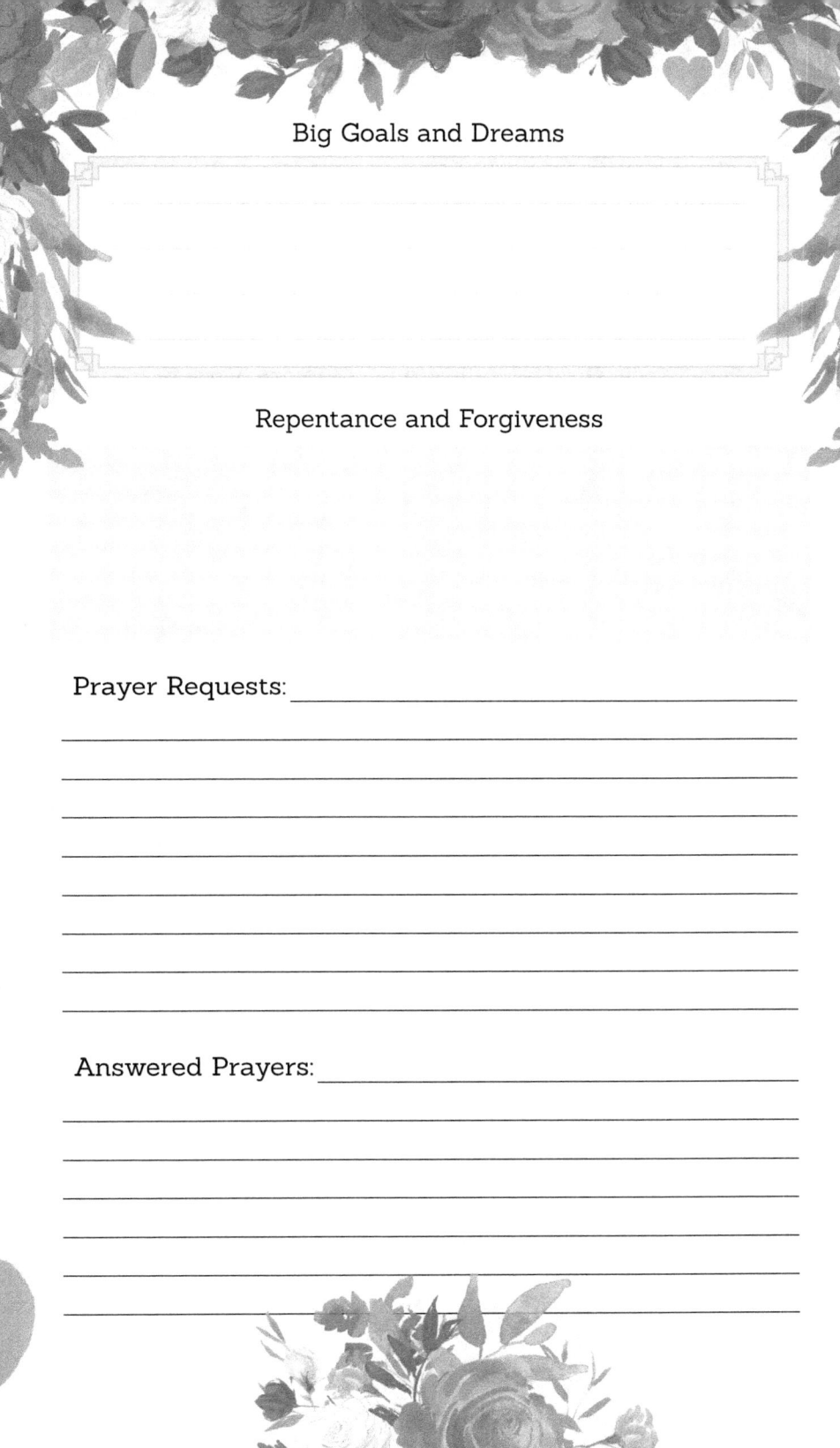

Big Goals and Dreams

Repentance and Forgiveness

Prayer Requests: _____

_____
_____
_____
_____
_____
_____
_____
_____

Answered Prayers: _____

_____
_____
_____
_____
_____
_____

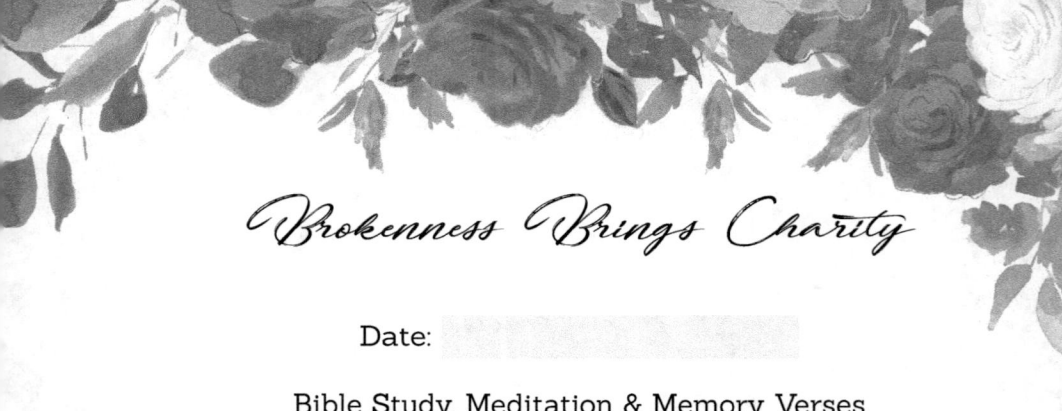

Brokenness Brings Charity

Date: _____

Bible Study, Meditation & Memory Verses

Gratitude & Praise to God: _____
_____
_____
_____
_____
_____
_____
_____

Brokenness Reflections

Big Goals and Dreams

Repentance and Forgiveness

Prayer Requests: _____
_____
_____
_____
_____
_____
_____
_____
_____

Answered Prayers: _____
_____
_____
_____
_____
_____

Brokenness Brings Goodness

Date: _____

Bible Study, Meditation & Memory Verses

Gratitude & Praise to God: _____
_____
_____
_____
_____
_____
_____
_____
_____

Brokenness Reflections

Big Goals and Dreams

Repentance and Forgiveness

Prayer Requests: _____
_____
_____
_____
_____
_____
_____
_____
_____
_____
_____

Answered Prayers: _____
_____
_____
_____
_____
_____
_____

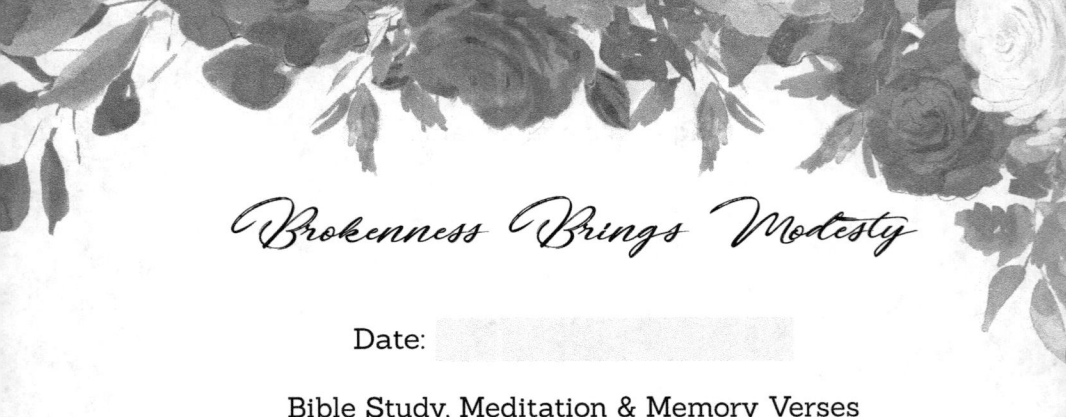

Brokenness Brings Modesty

Date: _____

Bible Study, Meditation & Memory Verses

Gratitude & Praise to God: _____

_____
_____
_____
_____
_____
_____
_____

Brokenness Reflections

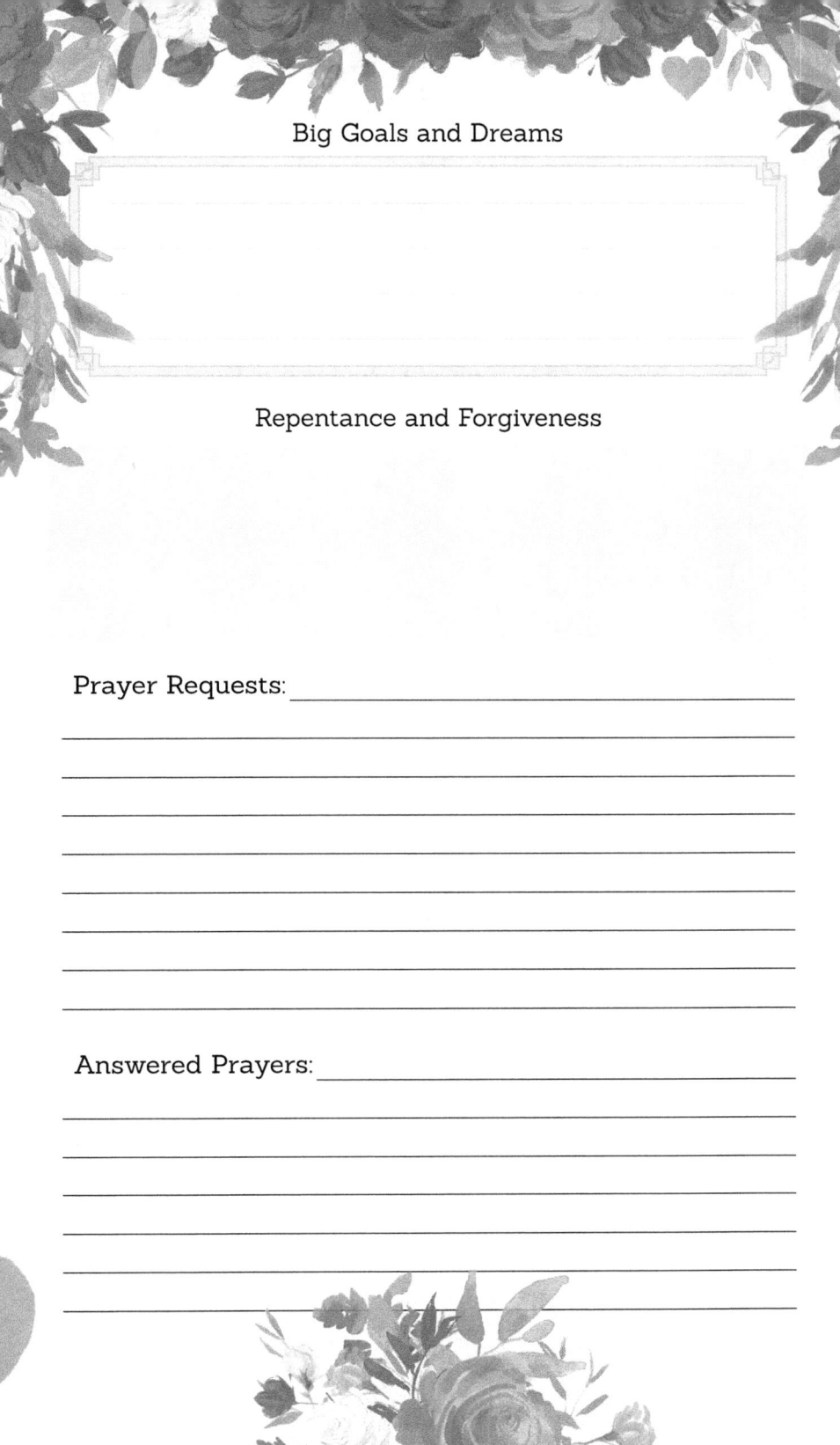

Big Goals and Dreams

Repentance and Forgiveness

Prayer Requests: _____

Answered Prayers: _____

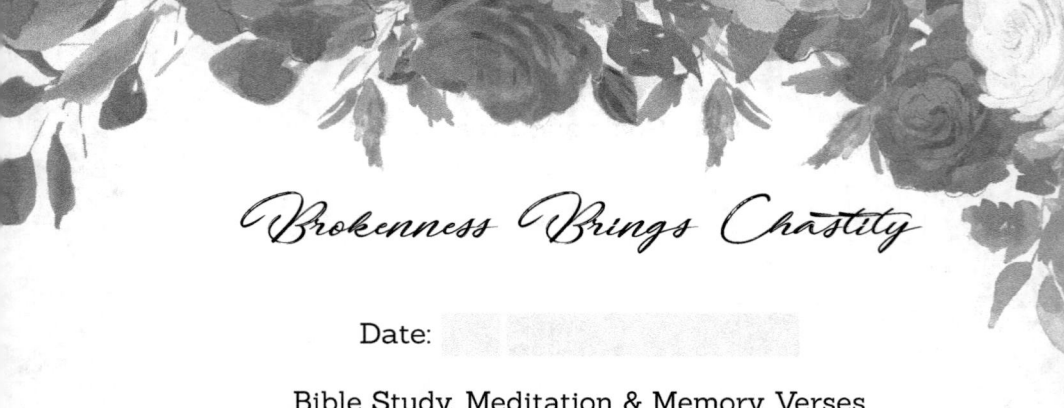

Brokenness Brings Chastity

Date: _____

Bible Study, Meditation & Memory Verses

Gratitude & Praise to God: _____
_____
_____
_____
_____
_____
_____
_____

Brokenness Reflections

Big Goals and Dreams

Repentance and Forgiveness

Prayer Requests: _____
_____
_____
_____
_____
_____
_____
_____
_____

Answered Prayers: _____
_____
_____
_____
_____
_____

Brokenness Brings Gentleness

Date: _____

Bible Study, Meditation & Memory Verses

Gratitude & Praise to God: _____
_____
_____
_____
_____
_____
_____
_____

Brokenness Reflections

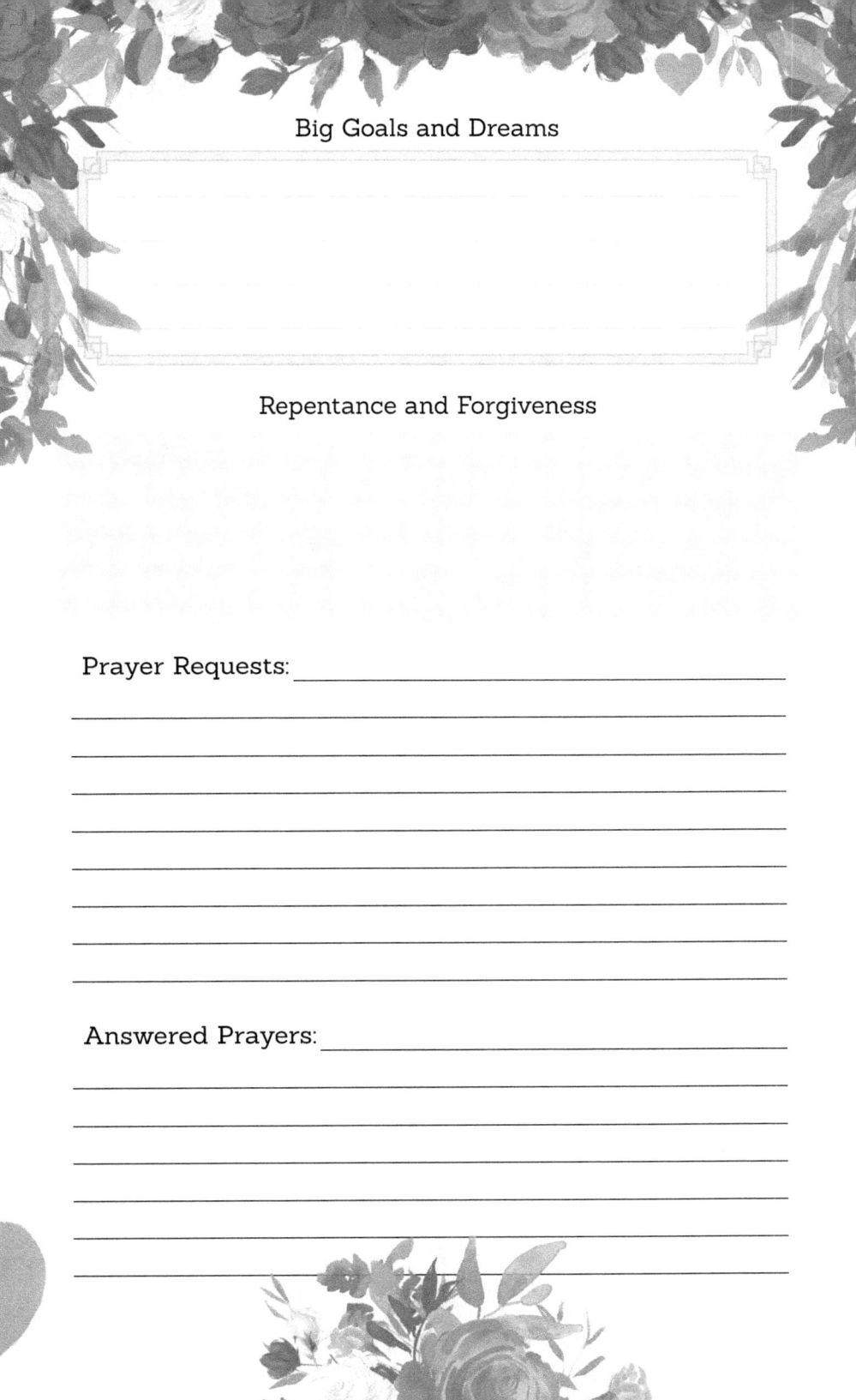

Big Goals and Dreams

Repentance and Forgiveness

Prayer Requests: _____
_____
_____
_____
_____
_____
_____
_____
_____

Answered Prayers: _____
_____
_____
_____
_____
_____

Brokenness Brings Boldness

Date: _____

Bible Study, Meditation & Memory Verses

Gratitude & Praise to God: _____
_____
_____
_____
_____
_____
_____
_____

Brokenness Reflections

Big Goals and Dreams

Repentance and Forgiveness

Prayer Requests: _____
_____
_____
_____
_____
_____
_____
_____
_____
_____

Answered Prayers: _____
_____
_____
_____
_____
_____
_____

Brokenness Brings Creativity

Date: _____

Bible Study, Meditation & Memory Verses

Gratitude & Praise to God: _____

_____
_____
_____
_____
_____
_____
_____

Brokenness Reflections

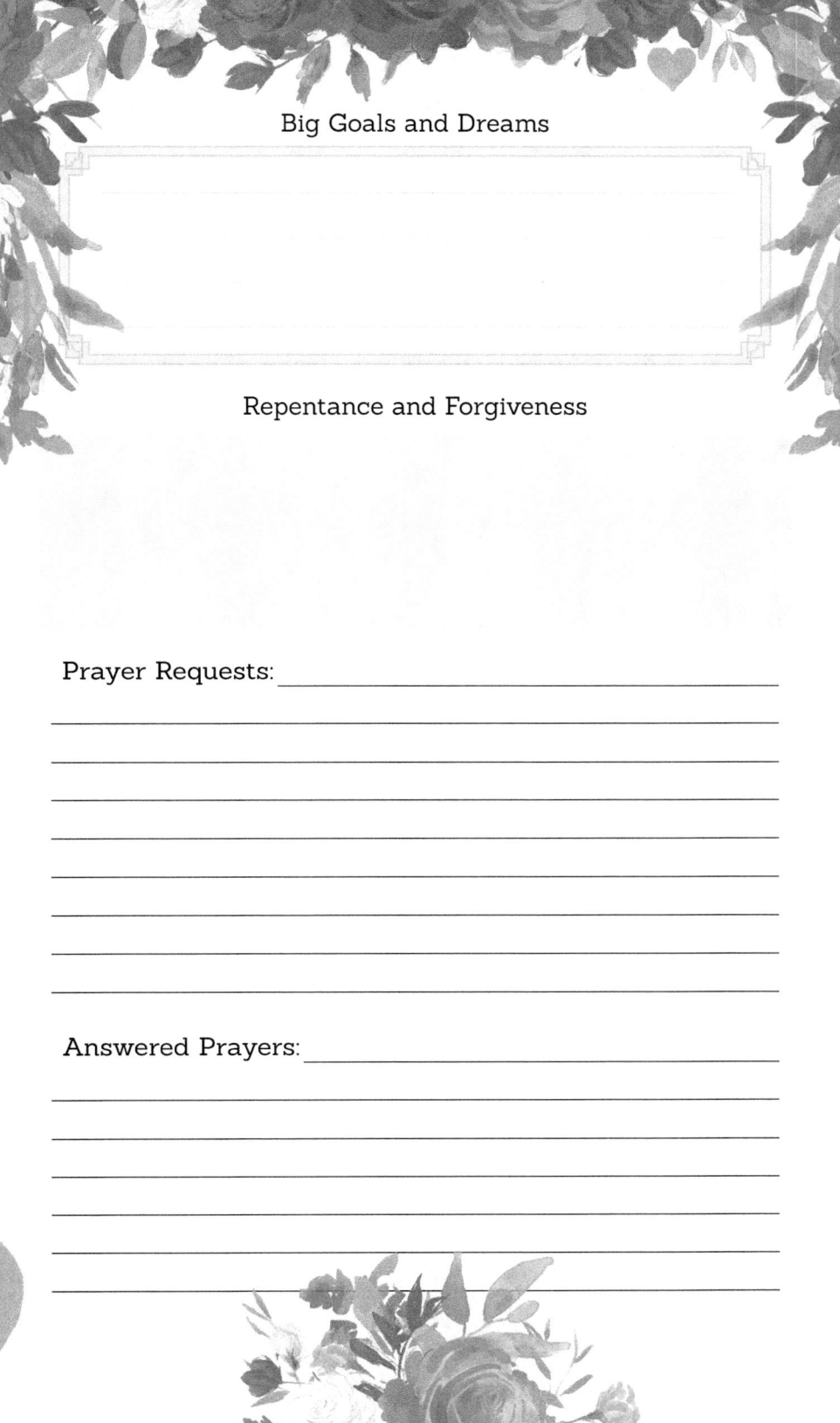

Big Goals and Dreams

Repentance and Forgiveness

Prayer Requests: _____

_____
_____
_____
_____
_____
_____
_____
_____
_____

Answered Prayers: _____

_____
_____
_____
_____
_____

Brokenness Brings Dependability

Date: _____

Bible Study, Meditation & Memory Verses

Gratitude & Praise to God: _____

_____
_____
_____
_____
_____
_____
_____
_____

Brokenness Reflections

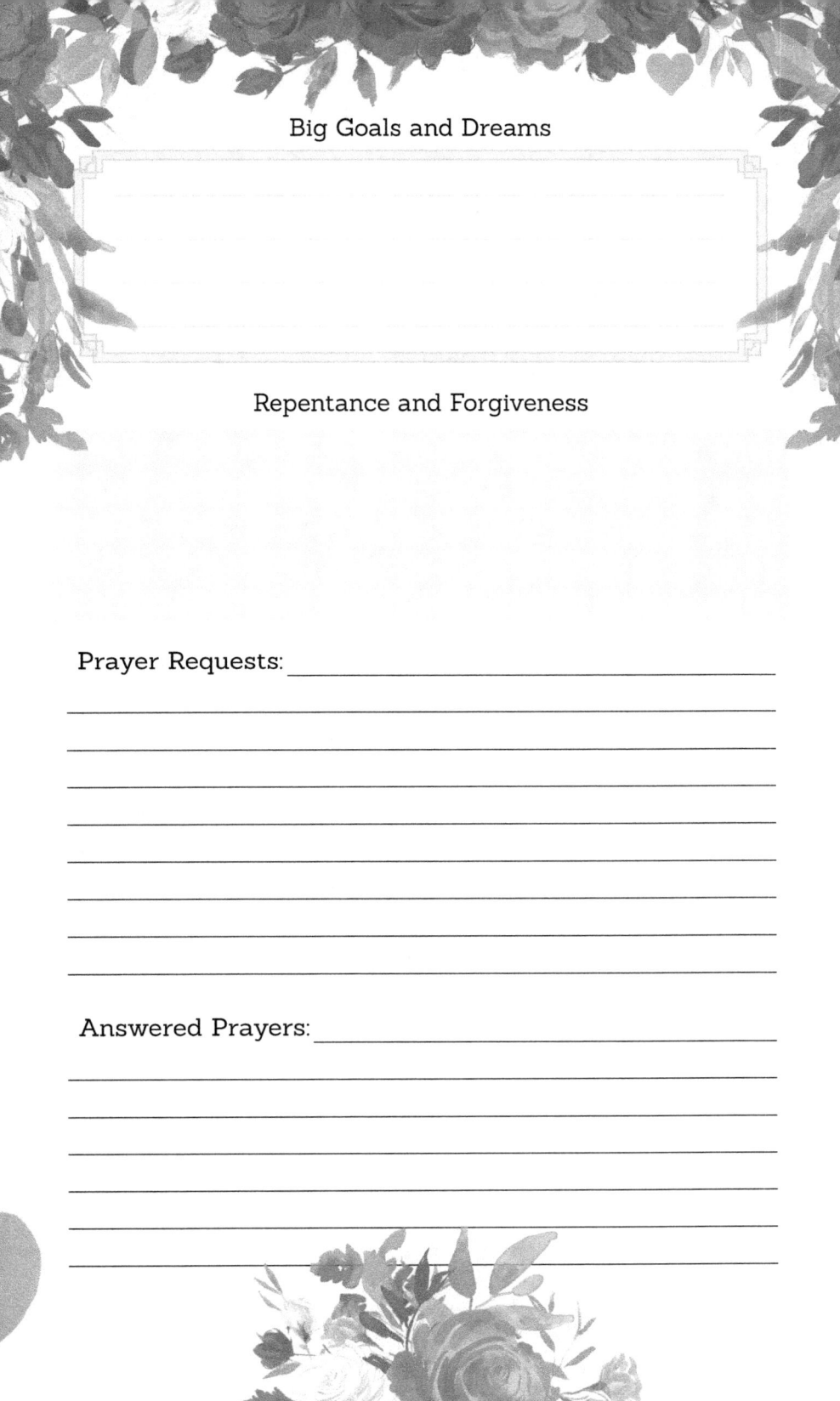

Big Goals and Dreams

Repentance and Forgiveness

Prayer Requests: _____

_____
_____
_____
_____
_____
_____
_____
_____
_____

Answered Prayers: _____

_____
_____
_____
_____
_____
_____

Brokenness Brings Endurance

Date: _____

Bible Study, Meditation & Memory Verses

Gratitude & Praise to God: _____
_____
_____
_____
_____
_____
_____
_____

Brokenness Reflections

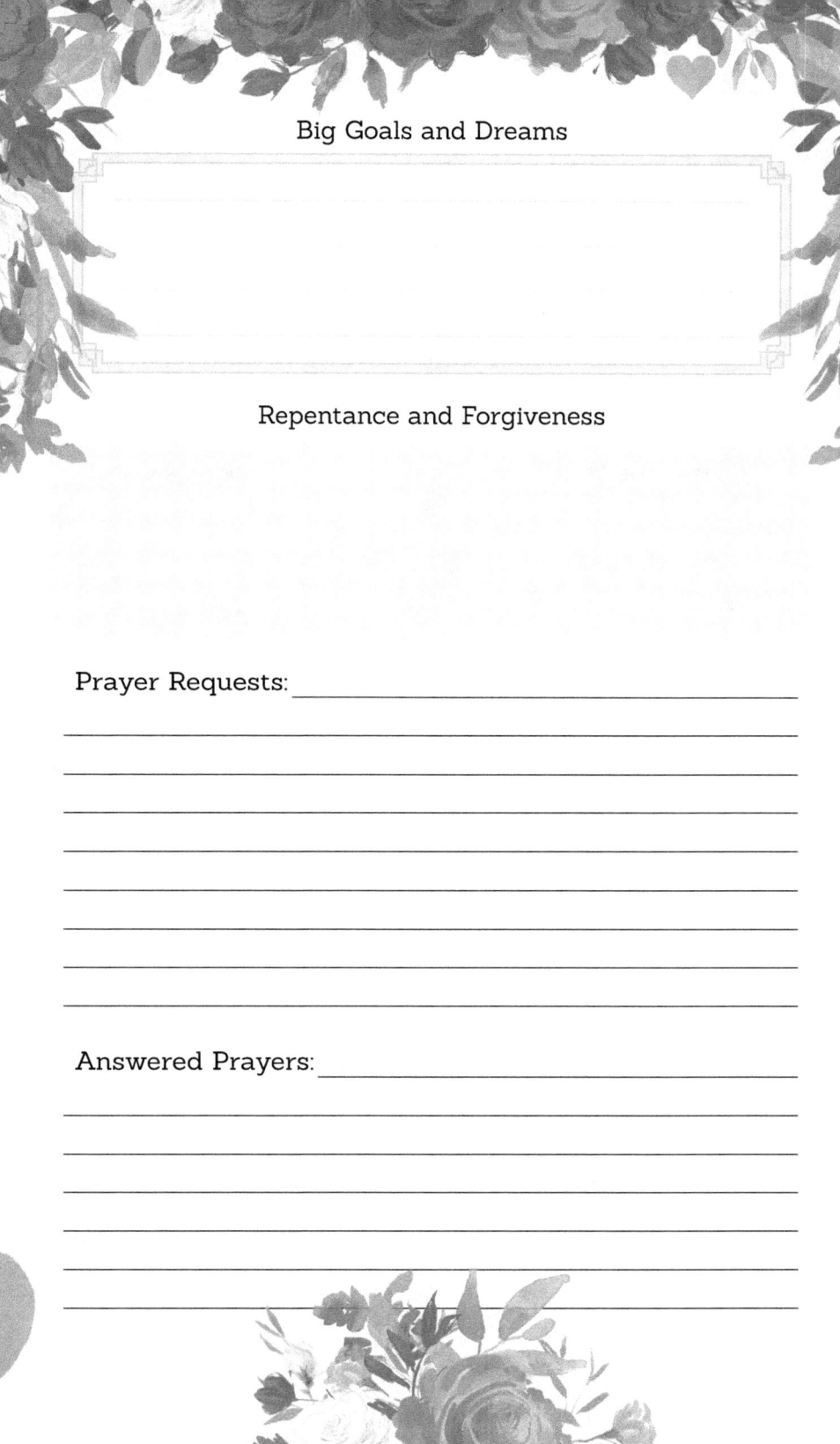

Big Goals and Dreams

Repentance and Forgiveness

Prayer Requests: _____
_____
_____
_____
_____
_____
_____
_____
_____
_____

Answered Prayers: _____
_____
_____
_____
_____
_____
_____
_____

Social Goal

Brokenness can be beautiful in your life.
Like a diamond shining bright

Start Date: _____ Achieve by: _____

Describe Your Social Goal

_____
_____
_____
_____
_____

Progress Check

_____
_____
_____
_____
_____

Actionable Steps

- ○ _____
- ○ _____
- ○ _____
- ○ _____
- ○ _____
- ○ _____

Reason for This Goal

_____
_____
_____
_____
_____

Challenges

Notes: _____
_____
_____
_____
_____
_____

Brokenness Brings Reverence

Date:

Bible Study, Meditation & Memory Verses

Gratitude & Praise to God: _____
_____
_____
_____
_____
_____
_____
_____

Brokenness Reflections

Big Goals and Dreams

Repentance and Forgiveness

Prayer Requests: _____
_____
_____
_____
_____
_____
_____
_____
_____
_____

Answered Prayers: _____
_____
_____
_____
_____
_____
_____

Brokenness Brings Hospitality

Date:

Bible Study, Meditation & Memory Verses

Gratitude & Praise to God: _____
_____
_____
_____
_____
_____
_____
_____
_____

Brokenness Reflections

Big Goals and Dreams

Repentance and Forgiveness

Prayer Requests: _____
_____
_____
_____
_____
_____
_____
_____
_____

Answered Prayers: _____
_____
_____
_____
_____
_____

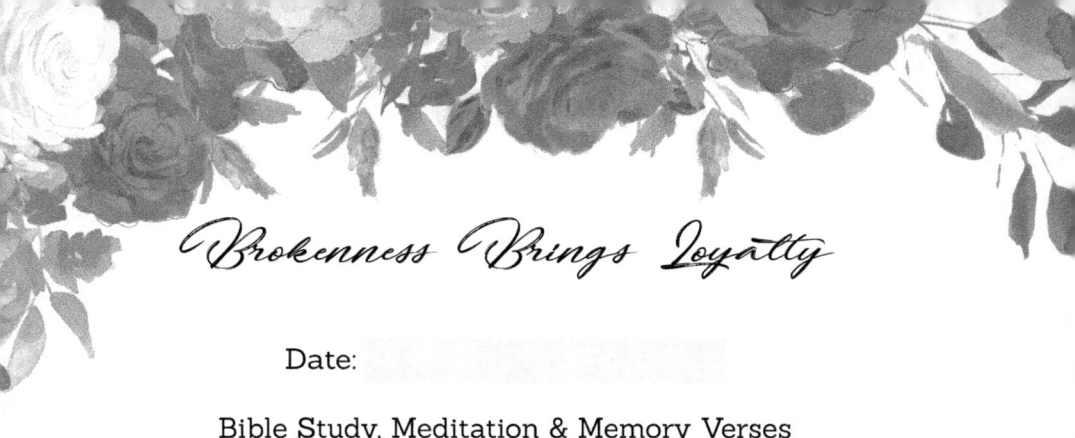

Brokenness Brings Loyalty

Date:

Bible Study, Meditation & Memory Verses

Gratitude & Praise to God: _____
_____
_____
_____
_____
_____
_____
_____

Brokenness Reflections

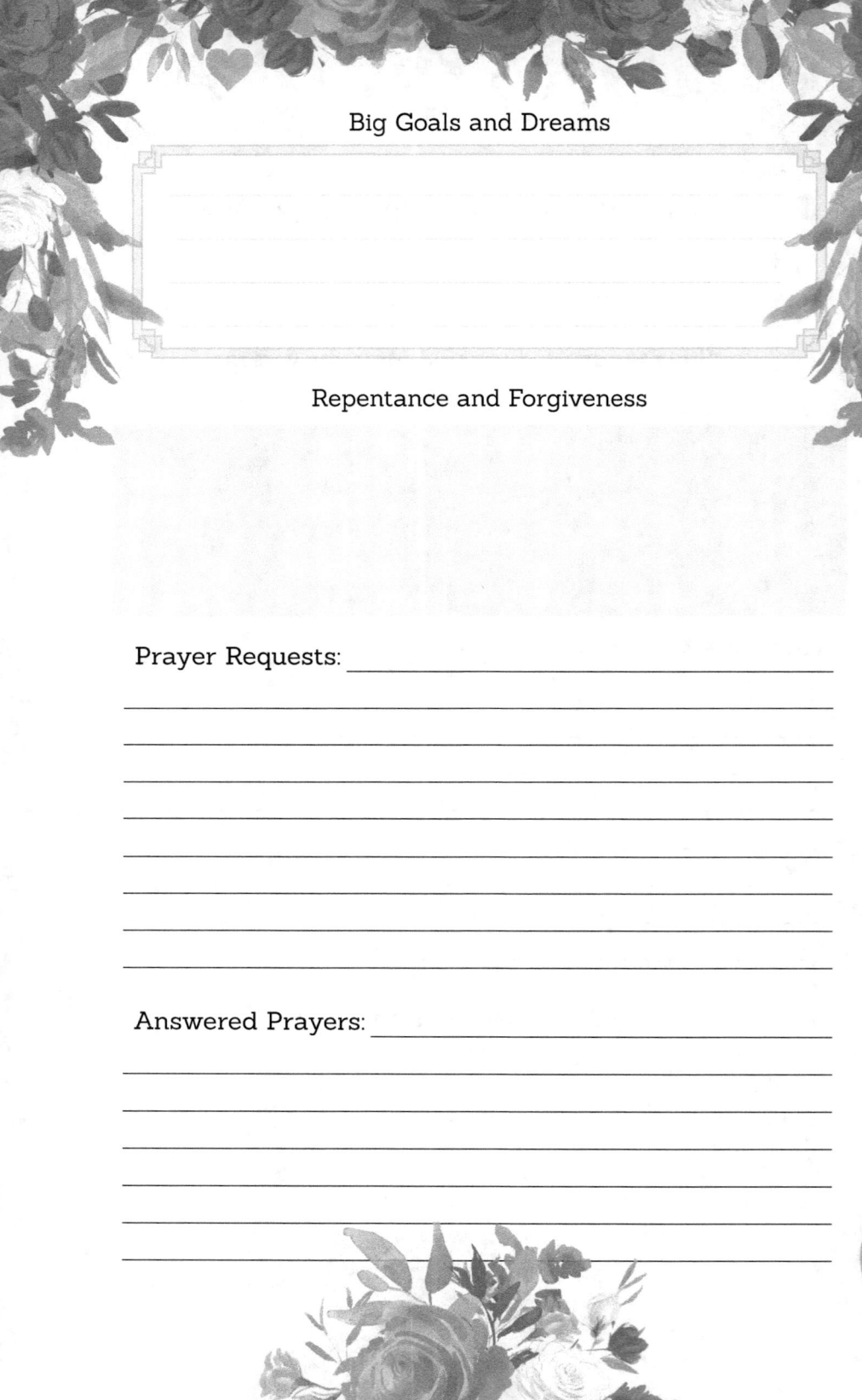

Big Goals and Dreams

Repentance and Forgiveness

Prayer Requests: _____
_____
_____
_____
_____
_____
_____
_____
_____

Answered Prayers: _____
_____
_____
_____
_____
_____
_____
_____

Brokenness Brings Security

Date:

Bible Study, Meditation & Memory Verses

Gratitude & Praise to God: _____
_____
_____
_____
_____
_____
_____
_____

Brokenness Reflections

Big Goals and Dreams

Repentance and Forgiveness

Prayer Requests: _____

_____
_____
_____
_____
_____
_____
_____
_____
_____

Answered Prayers: _____

_____
_____
_____
_____
_____
_____
_____
_____

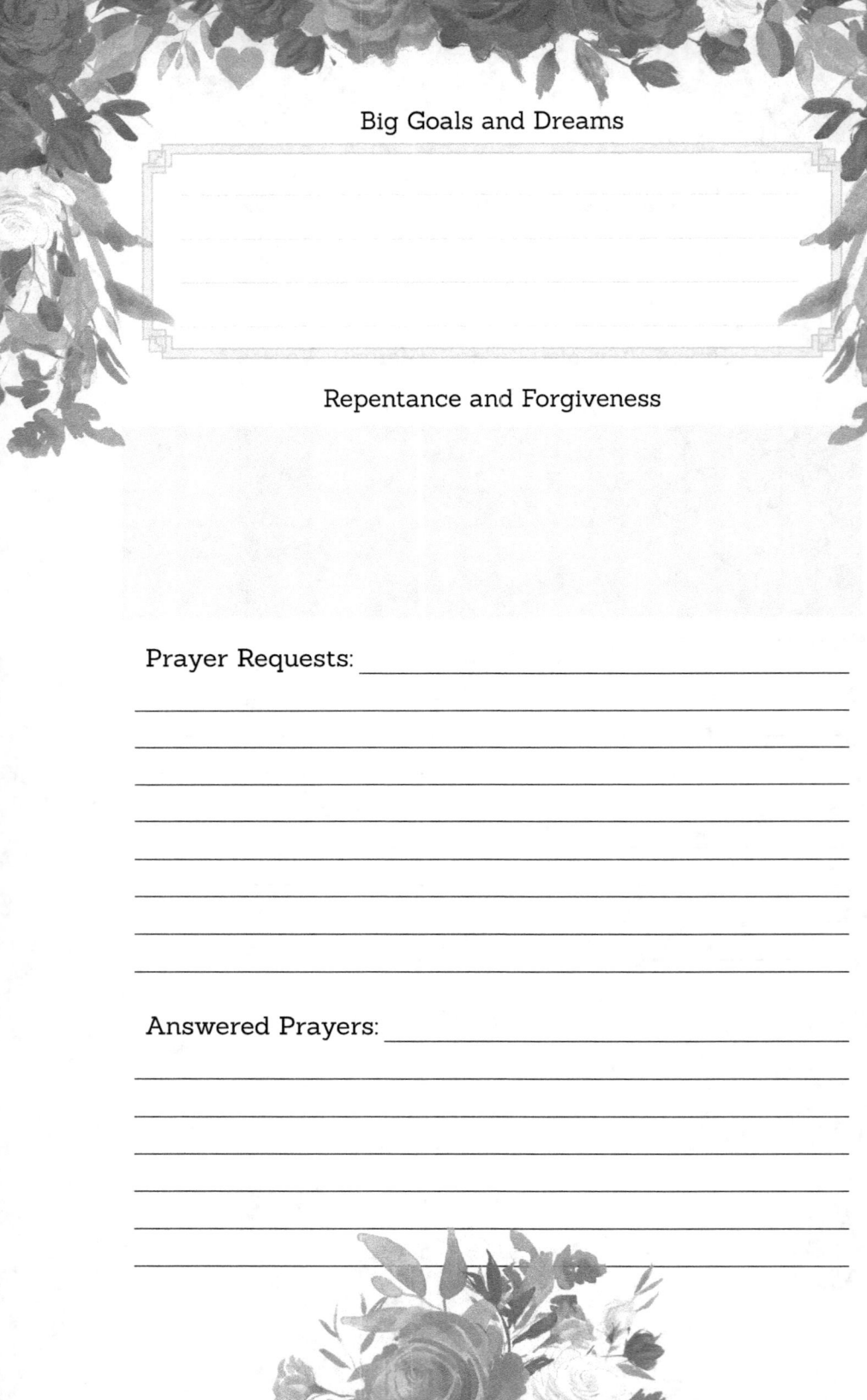

Brokenness Brings Sincerity

Date:

Bible Study, Meditation & Memory Verses

Gratitude & Praise to God: _____
_____
_____
_____
_____
_____
_____
_____
_____

Brokenness Reflections

Big Goals and Dreams

Repentance and Forgiveness

Prayer Requests: _____
_____
_____
_____
_____
_____
_____
_____
_____
_____

Answered Prayers: _____
_____
_____
_____
_____
_____
_____

Brokenness Brings Tolerance

Date:

Bible Study, Meditation & Memory Verses

Gratitude & Praise to God: _____
_____
_____
_____
_____
_____
_____
_____
_____

Brokenness Reflections

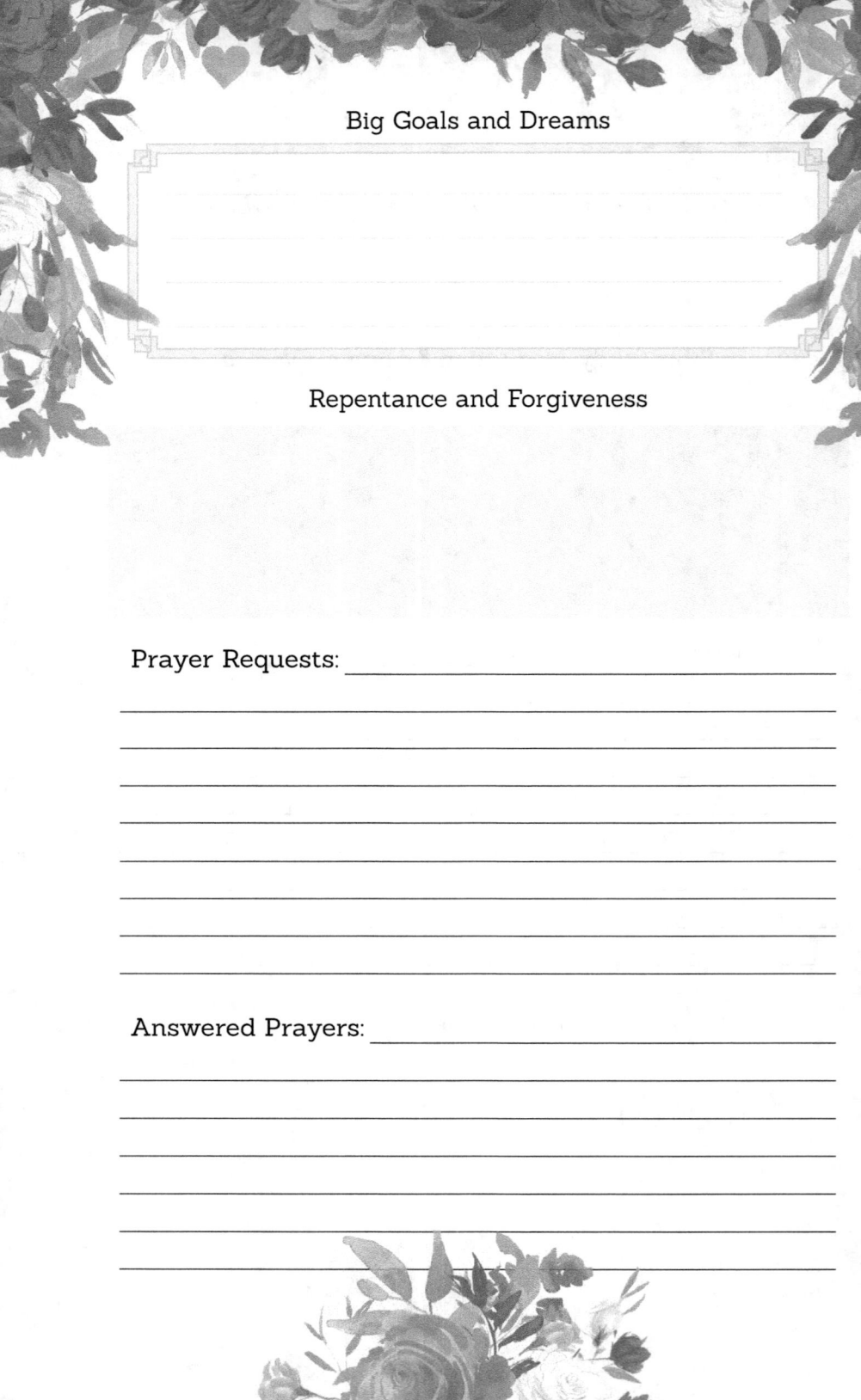

Big Goals and Dreams

Repentance and Forgiveness

Prayer Requests: _____

_____
_____
_____
_____
_____
_____
_____
_____
_____

Answered Prayers: _____

_____
_____
_____
_____
_____
_____
_____

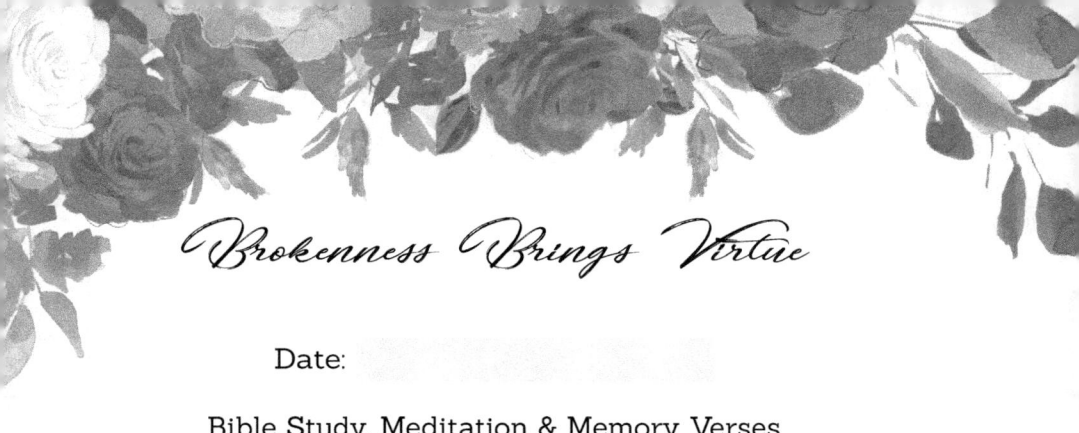

Brokenness Brings Virtue

Date:

Bible Study, Meditation & Memory Verses

Gratitude & Praise to God: _____
_____
_____
_____
_____
_____
_____
_____
_____

Brokenness Reflections

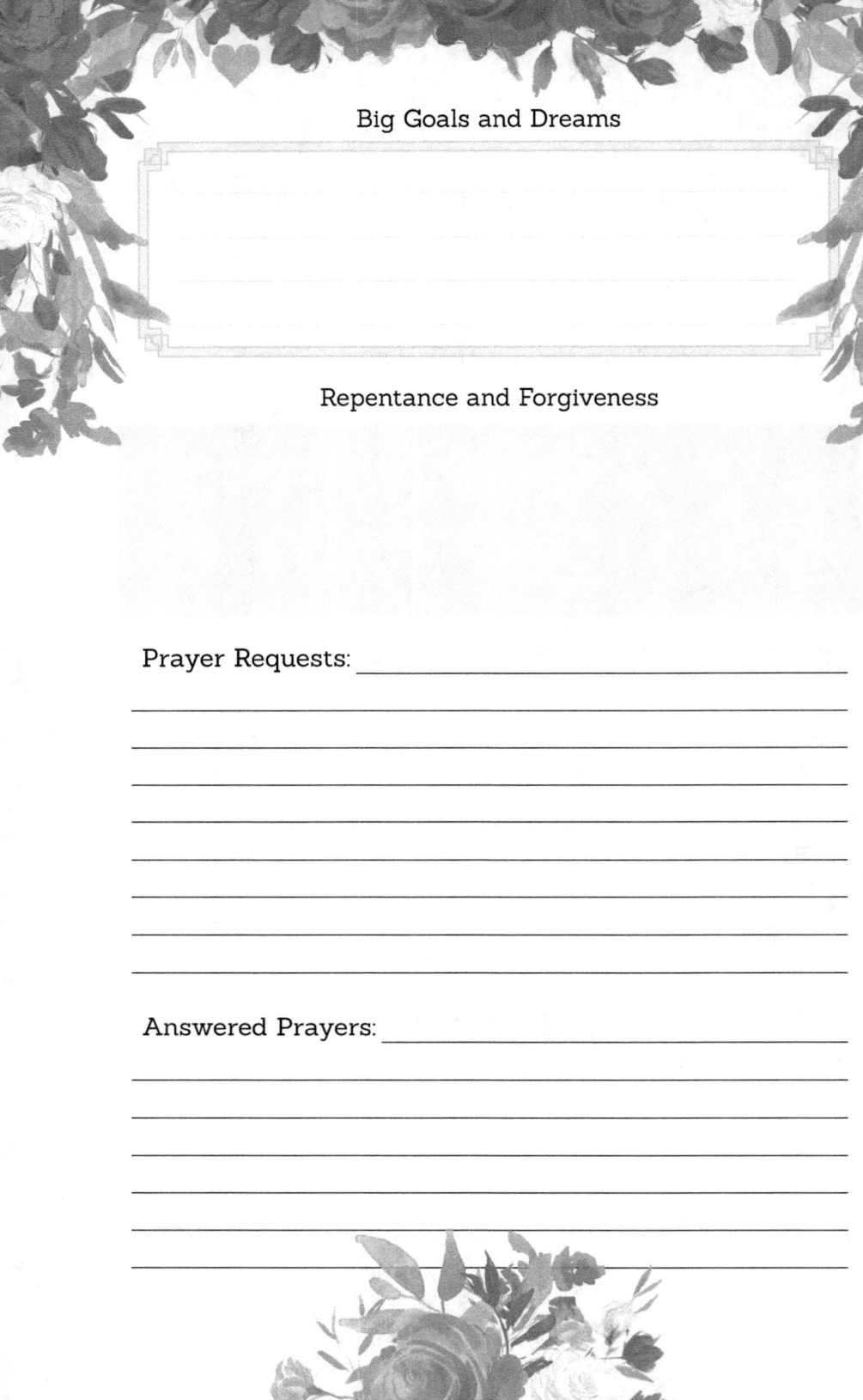

Big Goals and Dreams

Repentance and Forgiveness

Prayer Requests: _____

_____
_____
_____
_____
_____
_____
_____
_____

Answered Prayers: _____

_____
_____
_____
_____
_____
_____

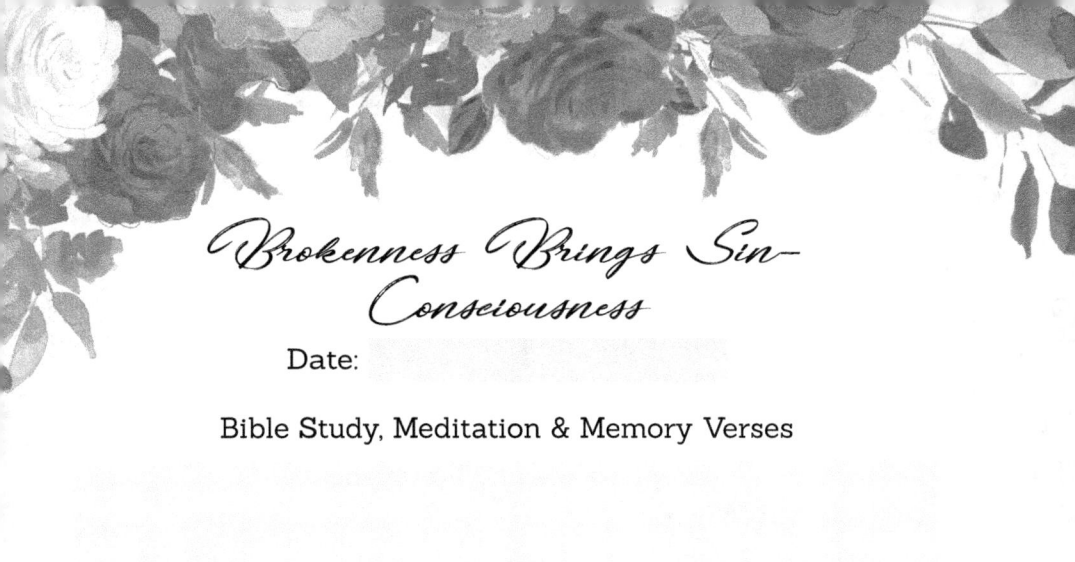

Brokenness Brings Sin-Consciousness

Date:

Bible Study, Meditation & Memory Verses

Gratitude & Praise to God: _____
_____
_____
_____
_____
_____
_____
_____
_____

Brokenness Reflections

Big Goals and Dreams

Repentance and Forgiveness

Prayer Requests: _____
_____
_____
_____
_____
_____
_____
_____
_____
_____

Answered Prayers: _____
_____
_____
_____
_____
_____
_____

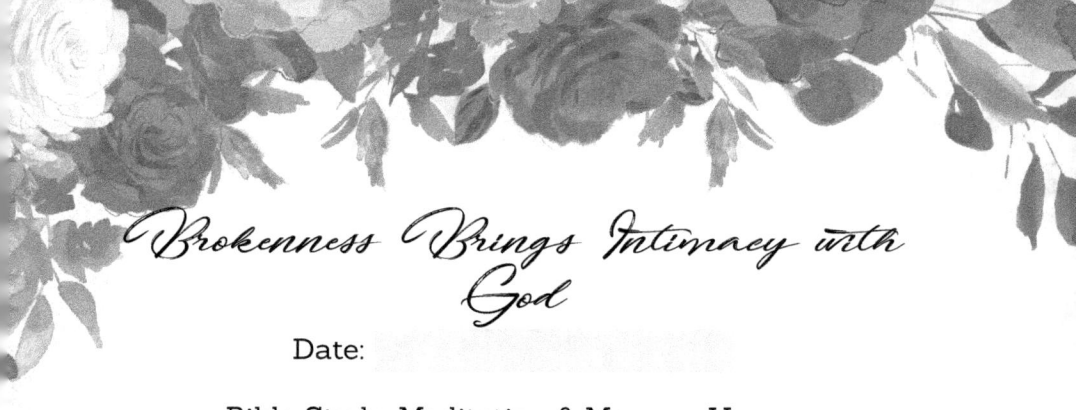

Brokenness Brings Intimacy with God

Date:

Bible Study, Meditation & Memory Verses

Gratitude & Praise to God: _____
_____
_____
_____
_____
_____
_____
_____
_____

Brokenness Reflections

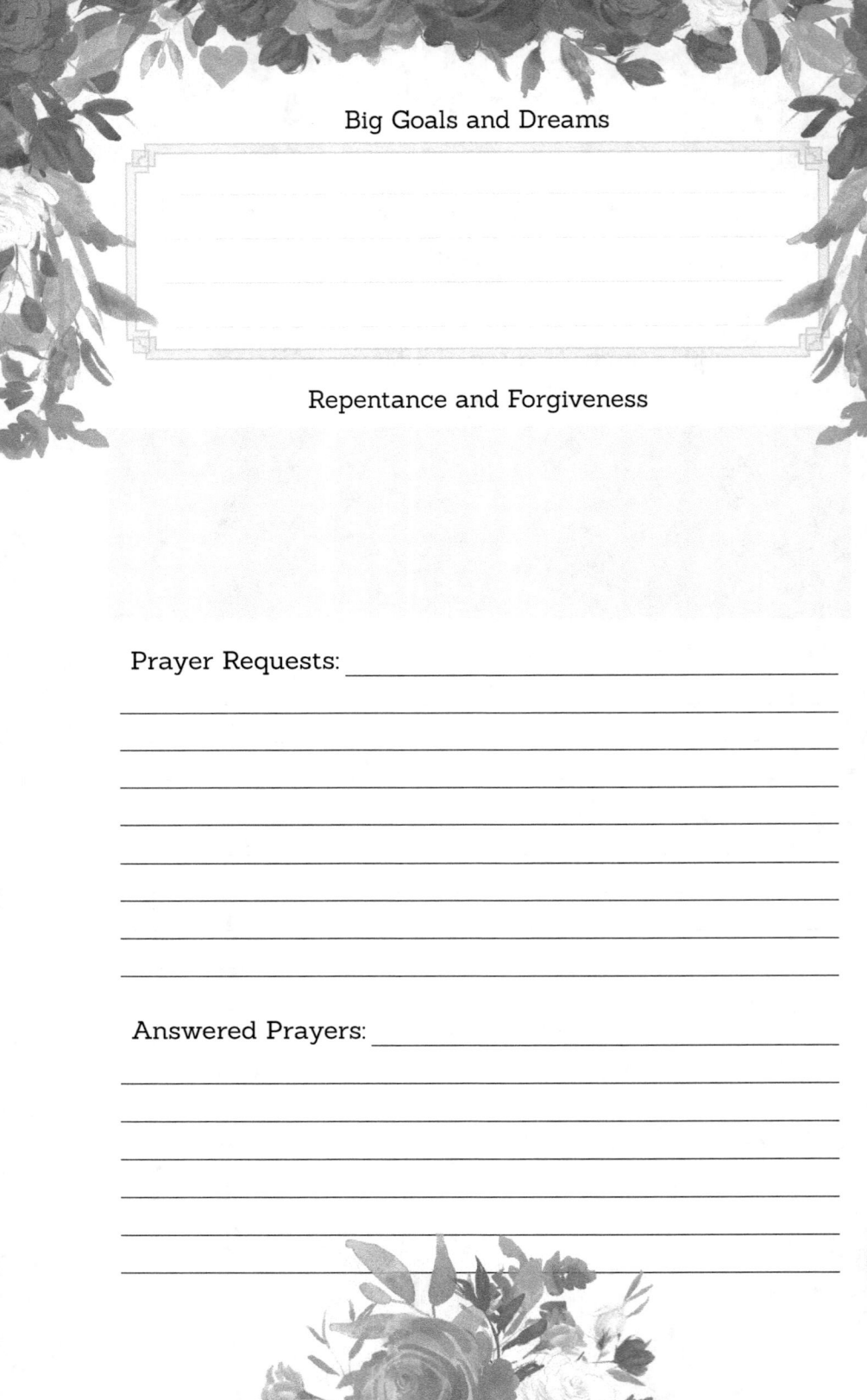

Big Goals and Dreams

Repentance and Forgiveness

Prayer Requests: _____

Answered Prayers: _____

Brokenness Brings Blessedness

Date: _____

Bible Study, Meditation & Memory Verses

Gratitude & Praise to God: _____

_____
_____
_____
_____
_____
_____
_____

Brokenness Reflections

Big Goals and Dreams

Repentance and Forgiveness

Prayer Requests: _____
_____
_____
_____
_____
_____
_____
_____
_____
_____

Answered Prayers: _____
_____
_____
_____
_____
_____
_____

Brokenness Brings Value

Date:

Bible Study, Meditation & Memory Verses

Gratitude & Praise to God: _____

_____
_____
_____
_____
_____
_____
_____
_____

Brokenness Reflections

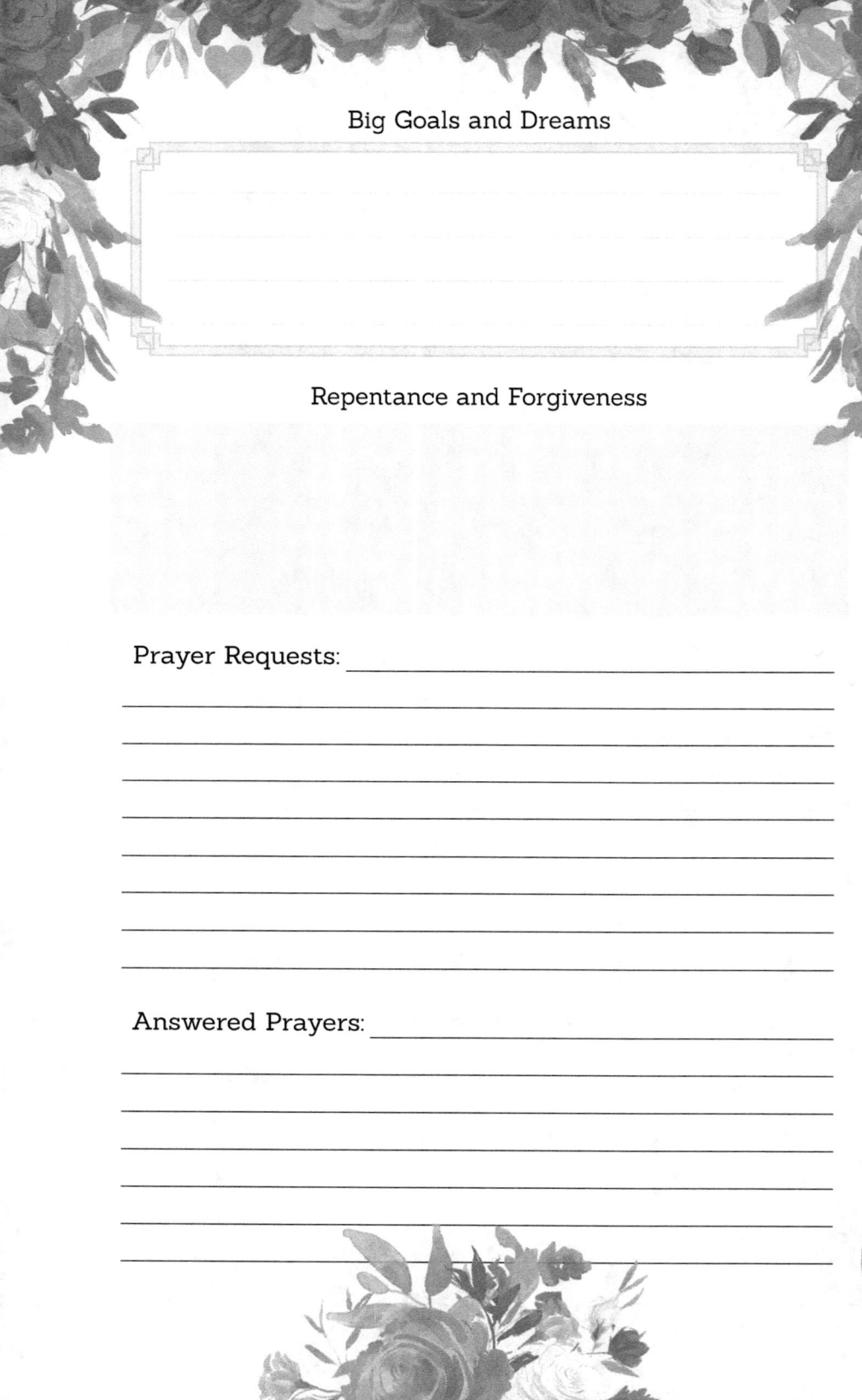

Big Goals and Dreams

Repentance and Forgiveness

Prayer Requests: _____
_____
_____
_____
_____
_____
_____
_____
_____
_____

Answered Prayers: _____
_____
_____
_____
_____
_____
_____
_____

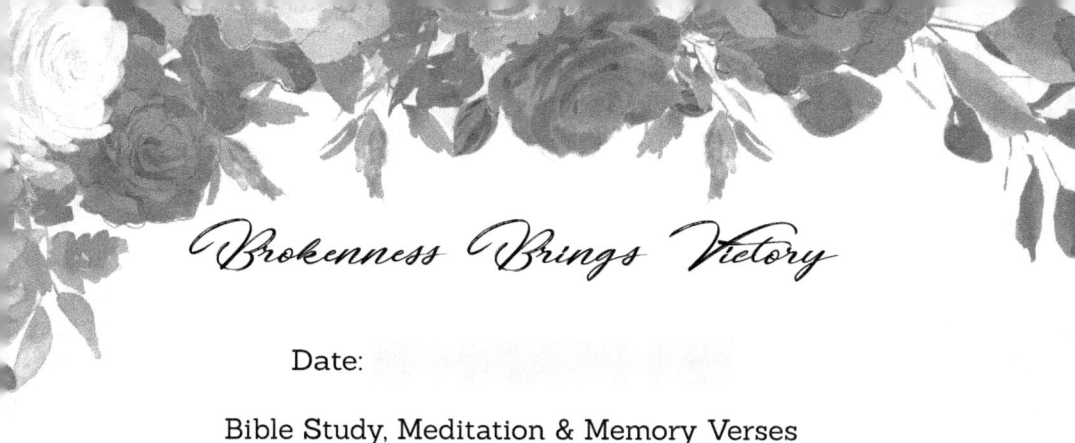

Brokenness Brings Victory

Date:

Bible Study, Meditation & Memory Verses

Gratitude & Praise to God: _____
_____
_____
_____
_____
_____
_____
_____
_____

Brokenness Reflections

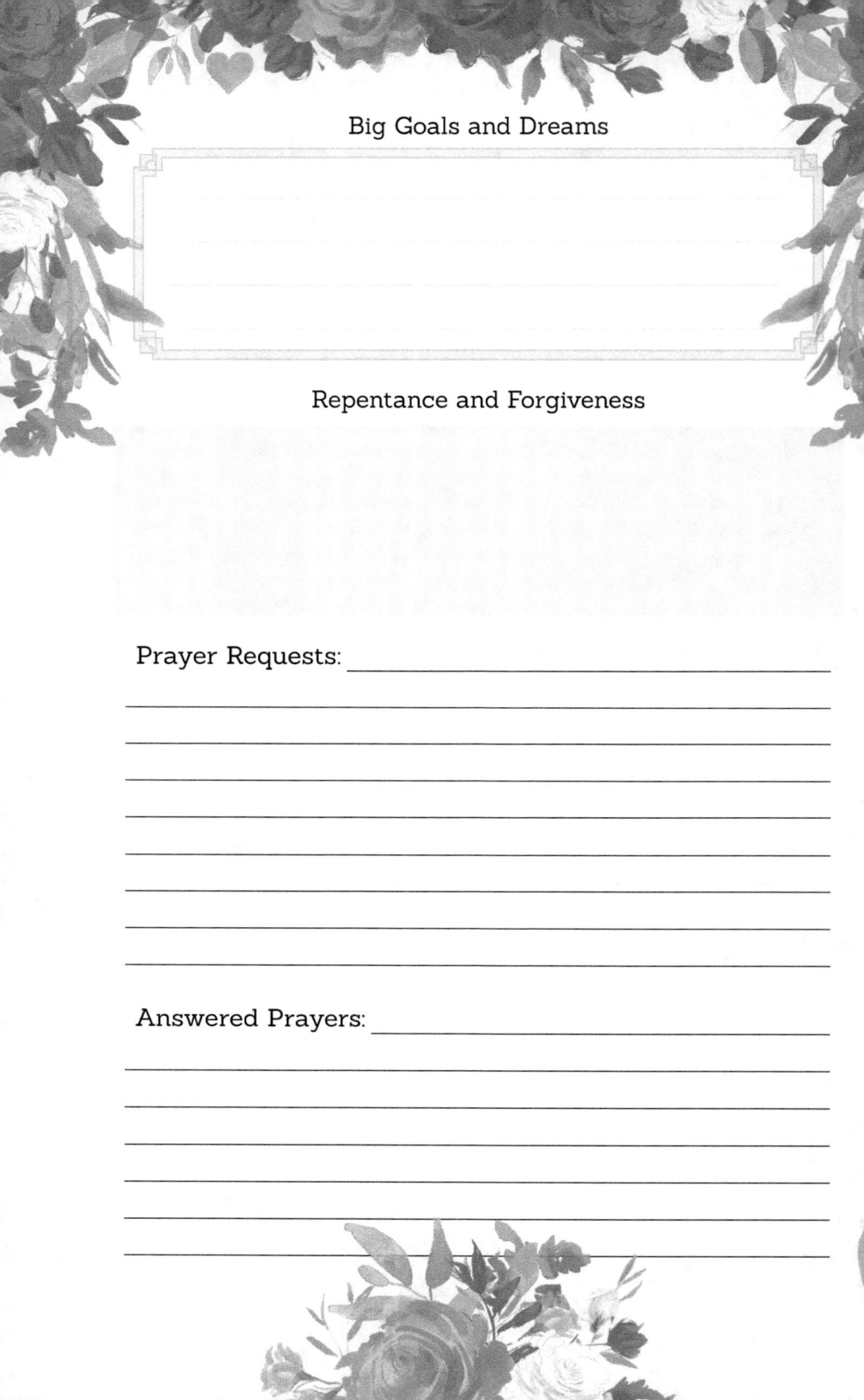

Big Goals and Dreams

Repentance and Forgiveness

Prayer Requests: _____

_____
_____
_____
_____
_____
_____
_____
_____
_____

Answered Prayers: _____

_____
_____
_____
_____
_____
_____
_____

Brokenness Brings Holiness

Date:

Bible Study, Meditation & Memory Verses

Gratitude & Praise to God: _____

_____
_____
_____
_____
_____
_____
_____

Brokenness Reflections

Big Goals and Dreams

Repentance and Forgiveness

Prayer Requests: _____

_____
_____
_____
_____
_____
_____
_____
_____
_____

Answered Prayers: _____

_____
_____
_____
_____
_____
_____
_____

Lifestyle Goal

Brokenness brings God's sheep back into His loving arms.

Start Date: Achieve by:

Describe Your Lifestyle Goal

_____
_____
_____
_____

Progress Check

Actionable Steps

- ○
- ○
- ○
- ○
- ○
- ○

Reason for This Goal

_____
_____
_____
_____
_____

Challenges

Notes: _____
_____
_____
_____
_____
_____

About the Author

Evangelist Katherine Elam Simpson was born and raised in the inner city of Watts, Los Angeles. Her childhood was filled with difficult times. Still wounded and hurting from her childhood trauma, Katherine became involved in a lifestyle that nearly killed her.

Katherine rededicated her life to the Lord and enrolled in the Saints of Value World Ministries Training Center, where she graduated as an ordained minister. Continuing her education at Esther Mallett International Bible University in 2002, Katherine graduated with a Bachelor of Arts degree in biblical theology.

Katherine is a vibrant and charismatic minister. She is noted for her soul-stirring messages and practical application of Christian principles. Through her evangelistic messages at church events, revivals, women's conferences, and Sunday morning worship services as the co-pastor of New Region For Christ, the Lord uses her to preach the gospel to hurting, neglected, and spiritually dying people.

Aside from her ministerial duties, Katherine is the proud wife of Pastor LaFrance Simpson. Together they are the parents of five wonderful children. She is also the founder of Women Waving the Banner of Freedom (WWTBOF) and the author of *Broken Beyond Recognition*.

Connect with Katherine

Email: Kgirls4@icloud.com
Instagram: firstladyksimpson
Facebook: Katherine Elam Simpson

www.ingramcontent.com/pod-product-compliance
Lightning Source LLC
LaVergne TN
LVHW051559070426
835507LV00021B/2661